Thinking Gorillas

Testing and Teaching
the Greatest Ape

BY BETTYANN KEVLES

illustrated with photographs

When gorillas were first captured, most did not survive. So Westerners had few chances to study them.

Then in 1925 a young female gorilla named Congo arrived safely in America. The famous psychologist Robert Mearns Yerkes was invited to study her, and he conducted the first serious inquiry into the gorilla mind.

In recent years gorilla studies have flourished in zoos and laboratories in the United States and Europe. And careful observations of wild gorillas are conducted in Africa, where the gorilla population has dwindled alarmingly.

Thinking Gorillas tells the stories of individual animals tested and even taught by dedicated, enthusiastic researchers. And it leads the reader to wonder what the future will reveal about the mental abilities of these intelligent—and endangered—apes.

Thinking Gorillas

Thinking Gorillas

Testing and Teaching the Greatest Ape

BY BETTYANN KEVLES

illustrated with photographs   E. P. Dutton   New York

For Sondra, who is also a good friend

title page photograph: *Bongo,*
an adult female gorilla (Margaret Redshaw)

Library of Congress Cataloging in Publication Data

Kevles, Bettyann.   Thinking gorillas.
Includes index.   Bibliography: p.
1. Gorillas—Psychology.   2. Animal intelligence.
3. Learning in animals.   4. Mammals—Psychology.   I. Title.
QL737.P96K38   1979   599'.88   79-12782   ISBN: 0-525-41074-0

Published in the United States by E. P. Dutton, a Division
of Elsevier-Dutton Publishing Company, Inc., New York

Published simultaneously in Canada by Clarke,
Irwin & Company Limited, Toronto and Vancouver

Editor: Ann Troy   Designer: Patricia Lowy

Printed in the U.S.A.   First Edition   10 9 8 7 6 5 4 3 2 1

AUTHOR'S NOTE

These stories are true, and many of the animals are still alive in different parts of the world. Each study is important because it reveals something about the gorilla mind. Together, they open a window into the world of humankind's closest animal relation.

ACKNOWLEDGMENTS

I could not have begun to tell these stories, both those that happened long ago and those that are not finished, without the cooperation of zoologists, primatologists, and psychologists in Great Britain, Spain, and the United States. Many provided me with reprints of their works. Others graciously escorted me through their facilities, and some were kind enough to look over parts of the manuscript.

I should like to thank Margaret Redshaw at University College, London, for introducing me to her subjects at the Jersey Wildlife Preservation Trust, and to Jeremy Mallinson and Jeremy Usher-Smith at the trust. I am also grateful to Molly Badham at the East Midland Zoological Society at Twycross, where I met Assumbo and Mamfe. I want to thank Prudence Napier at the British Museum of Natural History for her advice, and the Royal Geographical Society for information on Paul du Chaillu.

I am grateful to Cathy Garska and Edalee Harwell at the San Diego Zoo for their cooperation, and to Jim Dolan and Steven Joines at the Wild Animal Park. At the Los Angeles Zoo I want to thank Mike Crotty and Jean Crowell. Saul Kitchner and Dr. V. E. Moltram at the San Francisco Zoo provided information about Koko, as did Dr. Karl H. Pribram and Penny Patterson at Stanford University.

Arthur Riopelle was especially generous with information about Snowflake, as was Señor Jorge Sabater-Pi at the Barcelona Zoological Gardens. I am grateful to Ronald Nadler and Duane Rumbaugh at the Yerkes Regional Primate Center for providing me with reprints of their work.

Margaret Redshaw, Kelly Stewart, A. H. Harcourt, and Steven Joines also gave generously of their time in personal interviews, as did Penny Patterson and Arthur Riopelle on the telephone.

Thanks also to Julie Calvert for taking time from her own work on the lowland gorilla to look over the early chapters, and to Richard Dickerson for helping with the conclusion.

Mrs. Toby Pyle at the World Wildlife Federation generously sent me much useful information. And Edmund S. Munger kindly allowed me the run of the Africana Library at the California Institute of Technology. Thanks also to Jean Tatro at the Millikin Library at Caltech and to Ann Cain at the Pasadena Public Library for obtaining obscure and sometimes distant reference material.

I am grateful to Robert Huttenback for making space available for me to work at Caltech, and to Mary Doan for typing the manuscript.

Considerable critical help as well as enthusiasm came from Beth and Jonathan Kevles, and I received steady encouragement from my husband, Daniel, who has learned more about gorillas than he once believed possible.

CONTENTS

1	Beginnings	1
2	Fighting Joe	13
3	Papoose	26
4	Harcourt and Stewart with the Mountain Gorillas	37
5	Snowflake	47
6	Snowflake and Arthur Riopelle	56
7	Miss Congo	66
8	Miss Congo and Robert Yerkes	73
9	Assumbo and Mamfe	85
10	Assumbo, Mamfe, and Margaret Redshaw	94
11	Dolly	108
12	Ellie, Paki, and Patty Cake	117
13	Koko	127
14	Koko and Penny Patterson	136
15	The Future	150
	Bibliography	155
	Index	161

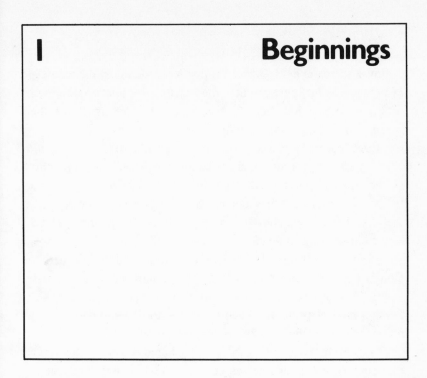

1   **Beginnings**

The giant silver-backed gorilla stopped at the edge of the cane field, stood upright, and then turned his massive head towards the forest. He nodded to those behind him, dropped down onto his powerful arms, and moved four-leggedly out into the field. A pair of young black-backed male gorillas responded to the signal and followed him out of the foliage into the sunlight. Soon two females emerged, one with a baby cupped to her breast. Finally, an infant scampered to catch up with the group.

Without pausing, they all went to work. Their great hands crushed the thick cane stalks so they could suck the sweet juices. As they feasted, they belly-rumbled pleasure sounds. Then the silverback stopped eating, barked abruptly, and moved out of the field and into the undergrowth.

The others stopped too, and followed obediently. They pushed through the tangled lianas until the silverback paused at a grassy clearing. Then they all sank down, pulled the grasses carelessly around themselves, and stretched out. Within moments all were asleep.

But in the cane field, African farmers raged amidst the wreckage of their crop. In a few minutes the gorillas had laid waste months of hard work. They berated themselves for letting down their guard. And they cursed *ngyulla*.

"Beware," they warned travelers to gorilla country. "*Ngyulla* is crafty and dangerous. And he is patient too. He waits crouching in the low branches of the musanga tree until a human passes below. Then he stretches out his hairy legs and, using his great feet like hands, snatches the passerby from the ground—and silently chokes him to death."

Stories like this one of man-killing gorillas used to flow with the Congo River through the lowlands of western Africa. Of course, no traveler ever saw an ambush. It never happened. But the story holds a kind of truth. For each time that gorillas rampage through a farmer's crop, they choke off his livelihood.

For eons, humans and gorillas have shared the enormous forests that stretch like a sash across central Africa. It is likely that ape ancestors (*Dryopithecus*) and our own hominid ancestors both roamed what is now central Africa about 14 million years ago.

And it is likely that these earlier animals avoided each other just as today's humans and gorillas do. Humans are wary of the frightening giants, and gorillas fear the human hunter.

Just when today's gorillas appeared is a mystery. Because gorillas have always lived in rain forests, where bones decay rapidly in the humid earth, they have left no fossil evidence. Very little is known about when the first gorillas separated from their pongid cousins the chimpanzees. We don't even know how much of Africa they inhabited when they were most abundant.

The earliest time that we can guess about is the Pleistocene age 2 million years ago. This was before the last of the great glaciers swept over countries north of Africa and changed the earth's climate as far south as the equator.

Lacking fossils, scientists have studied living gorillas in the hopes of discovering where their ancestors lived. An English primatologist, Colin Groves, traveled to 35 museums and collections all over Europe, the United States, and Africa. He examined and measured every single adult gorilla skull he could find and compared these 747 different skulls with what he knew about living gorillas.

He analyzed his data in terms of the ancient African landscape at the time when an enormous lake filled the whole Congo basin. Then geological upheavals opened a rift across all of equatorial Africa. This drained the lake into rivers and pushed up a chain of volcanoes: the Virungas in east Africa, and a smaller mountain range in the western Cameroons. Eventually a series of great lakes, including Lake Kivu and Lake Victoria, filled up some of the newly formed volcanic craters.

The gorillas probably appeared first in the eastern Congo at a time between glaciers when mountain forests spread all the way to the western coast. For ages, the climate alternated between glacial and interglacial periods. Over hundreds and thousands of years, the temperature fell about 5 degrees centigrade, and the whole life of the forest—what is called the *biome*—moved lower down the mountainside away from the cold.

When it was all over, the gorillas had broken into isolated and scattered groups. Those who had moved eastward were trapped at the new great lakes because they could not swim. Those who moved westward ranged all the way to the Atlantic Ocean in what are now the western lowland forests.

But the gorilla's deep barrel chest, his small ears, his large nostrils and shortened arms and legs, even his great size are typical adaptations for life in a cold climate. What is more, the gorilla's large teeth and enormous jaw muscles are best suited for eating the heavy vegetation that grows in mountain forests. They may be less useful to gorillas who live in the lowland forests, where they eat more fruit.

But these lowland gorillas have slowly adjusted to the warmer climate. They changed enough so that those taxonomists who specialize in classifying animals have placed them into separate species. Today all wild gorillas live in a wide band stretching across Africa that parallels the equator. Some live at sea level, and others in highlands up to 13,000 feet above the ocean.

Gorillas fall into three species. The most numerous, *Gorilla go-rilla gorilla,* wanders the rain forest of Africa from southeast Nigeria through Cameroon, Equatorial Guinea, Congo, Zaire, and Gabon and along the Congo River. Almost 800 miles to the east in central Africa, the eastern lowland gorilla, *Gorilla gorilla graueri,* lives in Zaire. And slightly eastward of them and higher up on the slopes of the Virunga volcanoes in Uganda, Rwanda, and Zaire, *Gorilla gorilla beringei* moves about in misty mountain forests.

All three species look very much alike. Only the length and color of their pelage, or hair, the width of their faces, the length of their arms and legs, and the shape of their nostrils tell the species apart. Without seeing members of the three species together, one can easily get them confused.

Until the twentieth century, taxonomists believed there was just one gorilla species, the lowland gorilla, the ones the explorers met

Looking out from Mount Mikeno, the home of the mountain gorilla (Courtesy of the American Museum of Natural History)

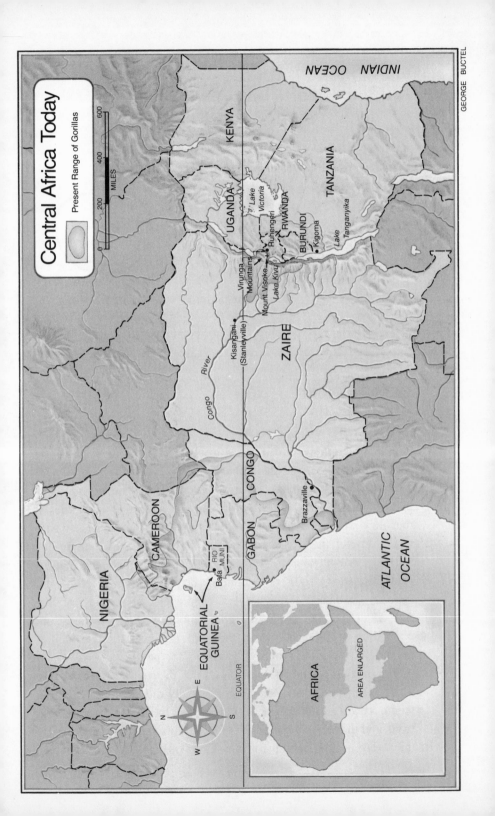

Central Africa Today

Present Range of Gorillas

MILES
0   200   400   600

GEORGE BUCTEL

INDIAN OCEAN

KENYA

UGANDA

Lake
Victoria

RWANDA
Ruhengeri
Virunga
Mountains
Mount Visoke
Lake Kivu

BURUNDI
Kigoma

TANZANIA

Lake
Tanganyika

ZAIRE

Kisangani
(Stanleyville)

Congo
River

CONGO

Brazzaville

GABON

CAMEROON

RIO
MUNI
Bata

EQUATORIAL
GUINEA

NIGERIA

ATLANTIC
OCEAN

EQUATOR

N
W   E
S

AFRICA

AREA ENLARGED

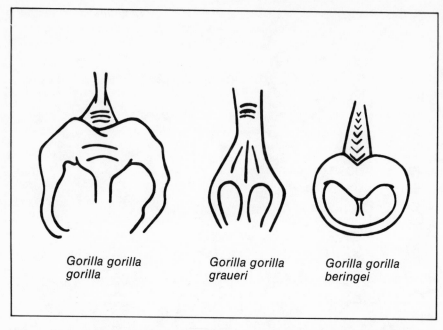

Nostril shapes of the three different gorilla species (Adapted from drawings by Don Cousins)

in the 1840s. Of all the gorillas, these live closest to large human populations, and it was a lowland gorilla that triggered the often repeated story of the ambush.

The Africans explained that *ngyullas* used to be people—lazy people who decided to let their hair grow all over their bodies so that they would not have to bother about making clothes or shelters. Some of the Africans said they were were-apes: human during the daylight hours and apes at night. Others believed that gorillas housed the souls of the uneasy dead. Some still believe that *ngyulla* has magic, especially in his fingers, toes, and testicles. And if these parts are separated from the rest of his body and cooked up in the right recipe, they provide great strength and supernatural powers to whoever swallows the potion.

Explorers repeated these stories as if they were trying to convince themselves that such creatures really did exist. By the nineteenth century, Europeans had relegated their own horrors, like trolls and dragons, to the pages of children's fairy tale books. Now they were on the lookout for new kinds of monsters.

The other great apes, the chimpanzee and the orangutan, had been familiar in Europe since the seventeenth century. Baby chimps and orangs had survived rough ocean voyages from Africa and the South Seas just long enough to prance in belled caps and velvet leggings around European courts. These playful babies mimicked people and were admired as cute, clownlike animals, curiously like ourselves.

But sadly for the gorilla, the Western world discovered it 200 years later at just the wrong moment in history. Rumors of a horrendous black ape had circulated for centuries. Hanno, an explorer from Carthage in the fifth century B.C., first described gorillas. But until the 1840s there was no proof that they existed.

At this time two Protestant missionaries, Reverend Thomas Savage and Reverend Wilson in Gabon, sent a pen-and-ink sketch of a gorilla to an anatomist, Dr. Jeffries Wyman, in America. Wyman forwarded the gorilla sketches to Dr. Richard Owen, a British anatomist. Owen soon obtained pieces of gorillas, skin and bones, and he managed to fit together a whole animal quite distinct from the chimpanzee.

By 1847, the gorilla had taken its place in the animal classification charts. It is a member of the superfamily Hominoidea, along with *Homo sapiens*. But it is in the family Pongidae, along with the chimpanzee and orangutan. It is always listed as species *Gorilla gorilla*.

Now solidly settled in the books, gorillas proved evasive in the flesh. Their health is delicate, and most captured gorillas simply did not survive. Westerners never got to see cuddly infant gorillas as they had seen the other apes as babies. Instead, Europeans and Americans met their first gorillas as exaggerated monster drawings in popular newsweeklies. Little wonder that the public greeted gorillas as phantoms out of some universal nightmare. They were, after all, huge, hairy, and black.

Black was not beautiful in the nineteenth century. Many Americans still owned African slaves, and they spoke about black people as inferiors in order to justify keeping them enslaved. The gorilla's black skin suggested that it was related to the African. And gorillas inherited all the scorn, the fantasy, and the fear that white people had heaped upon Africans.

Some white people reasoned that blacks were halfway between themselves and apes. They looked at the animal world as an organized place in which every animal and plant filled a special niche. They believed that the orders of life, which had been carefully set down by naturalists 100 years earlier, had always been that way. When they read the Bible, they accepted literally that all of the animals alive on earth in 1860 were exactly the same as those that lived in the Garden of Eden.

But a few people had begun to look at the natural world differently. Young Charles Darwin had roamed the English countryside, picking up odd bits of things he identified as fossils. As an adult, Darwin sailed around the world, gathering more specimens of past and living life-forms from remote islands and continents.

After years of pondering his collection, Darwin published his ideas in the *Origin of Species* and, later, in *The Descent of Man*. In the first book he explained that animal forms are always changing. In the second he discussed the similarities between human beings and apes by suggesting that we shared a common ancestor in the distant past.

Two years after Darwin's first book appeared, a popular explorer reached London with the stuffed body of an adult gorilla. He had deliberately posed the gorilla with a gruesome grin and hands outstretched as if about to strangle someone. Its appearance caused an uproar.

Journalists satirized the newfound ape by mimicking the abolitionists' slogan. Comparing the ape to black slaves, they had the gorilla ask, "Am I a man and a brother?" They saw evidence in the gorilla's hooded, sunken eyes that humans could not possibly share anything with it. They said that the soulless beast was proof that the devil lived on earth.

Yet when the uproar died down, Darwin's defenders felt that on the contrary, the discovery of the gorilla helped prove Darwin right. Here was an anthropoid—a manlike ape—similar to us in height and bearing—clearly a distant cousin.

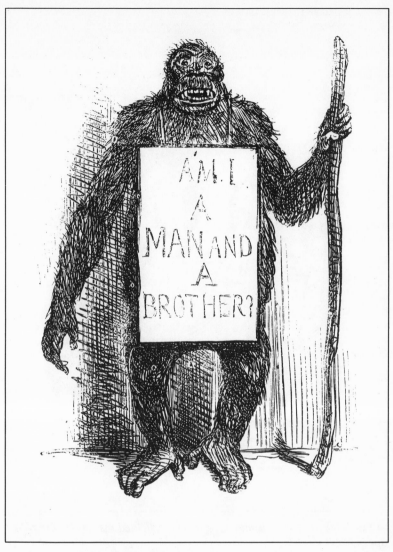

At the time of the United States' Civil War, Punch *drew a parallel between the controversy over the gorilla and the plight of the slave.* (Punch)

Whether they thought of gorillas as monsters or relatives, nineteenth-century explorers and scientists were off to Africa to hunt them. Some tried to get them alive because there were cages to fill in the great new gardens of the period: the living museum, the zoological garden—or zoo. But only a few gorillas lived through the ocean voyage; none long enough to make any difference to

THE LION OF THE SEASON.

Alarmed Flunkey. "MR. G-G-G-O-O-O-RILLA!"

In the 1860s, the British magazine Punch *ridiculed the newly discovered ape.* (Punch)

science. And zookeepers accepted as fact that it was impossible to keep a gorilla alive.

Most explorers never bothered to capture them at all. There was as great a market for dead apes as for live ones. Adventurers or scientists, and some people who were a little of both, invaded the area around the Congo River. Gorilla skins got top money, as did their bones. Even the story of a gorilla hunt had a price in the open market.

Gorillas live in groups. Shooting one usually meant killing the others. Babies, too small to put up a struggle, are the easiest to capture. But taking a baby almost always requires killing its mother first. In the past, and today as well, probably four gorillas died for each one captured alive.

The last 100 years have been hard on gorillas. Many have been slaughtered or captured. And those that remained in the wild found their dark rain forests exposed to explorers and later destroyed by farmers and loggers who, as Africa's human population rises dramatically, hunt them for food as well as for the forest space they occupy.

Gorillas are slow to adapt to change. They depend for food on the lush growth near the edges of forests. As those forests diminish, gorillas are squeezed into smaller patches of land.

From the many thousands of gorillas that probably lived 100 years ago, few of their descendants remain today. No one knows exactly how many there are. Estimates run from a few thousand lowland gorillas to only a few hundred of the mountain species. In 1973, a Convention on International Trade in Endangered Species met in Sweden. The participants drew up a list of the animals which will disappear altogether from the earth unless they are helped immediately. Gorillas are near the top of the list.

According to the convention, it is illegal to hunt gorillas or collect them without very special permission for a special purpose, usually a scientific one. Yet poaching goes on. Superstitious tribesmen still kill gorillas for their magical powers; in some places other tribesmen just plain hunt them for meat.

But gorillas have their human defenders too. In the forests of Uganda, Rwanda, Zaire, and Cameroon, scientists and conservationists from all over the world are taking censuses of the gorilla populations and are studying the way they fit into their complicated ecologies. By patient observation, they are slowly compiling a complete picture of how gorillas live when they are unmolested. Without this picture, the studies of psychologists in zoos and laboratories would be meaningless, for they would have no norm against which they could compare their discoveries.

While those who work in Africa fight desperately to preserve the separate gorilla species in their natural habitats, others have a grimmer outlook. They foresee the gorilla extinct in the wild by the end of this century. They are working to breed enough gorillas in captivity to keep them going, in the hope that one day they can return to a restored, natural homeland.

These scientists do not agree about what is best for gorillas. They do not agree about how intelligent gorillas are or even where they fit into the envolutionary picture. What they do share is an enthusiasm for these individual animals. Whether they are tracking gorillas in the wild, or testing and teaching them in zoos and laboratories, they develop an admiration that often becomes a passion for their gorilla friends.

2   **Fighting Joe**

High noon in the still west African summer, and no birds sang. A small gorilla crouched deep in a berry patch, picking his way through the tiny red fruits and stuffing them into his mouth. Then something disturbed him, and he began to cry for his mother. She sat several yards away, eating her own hoard of acid-sour fruits.

The young animal's cries, whines like those of a human child, broke the silence. They told a small party of men moving through the forest that gorillas were near. The men followed the sounds until they saw two sets of footprints that looked something like a cross between a human hand and foot.

The hunting party continued down a hill. In single file they balanced on a log to cross a stream, exactly as the gorillas must have crossed it earlier that morning. When they reached a huge granite boulder, they hid behind it so they could watch the animals.

One of the hunters loaded a double-barreled rifle. The only white man in the group, sheltered beneath a broad straw hat, whispered in his ear. Then the gunman led the party into the berry patch.

The mother gorilla grew wary. She stopped eating and rose to her full height. But before she could take a step, she caught a bullet in the center of her forehead. She fell forward then, face-down among the ripe berries.

The young gorilla could not have understood the gunshot noise or the strange new silence that filled the clearing. He ran to his mother and clung to her familiar black hairs for comfort. But his mother could no longer help him. He whimpered beside her until he saw humans walking towards him. Then he ran.

With his mother's blood covering his face, the small gorilla raced blindly to the nearest tree and scrambled up its trunk. When he could go no higher, he stopped, poised on a slender branch, and roared down at the men below. They moved backwards, beyond his range of vision, and the gorilla stayed on the limb.

When the men returned, the sturdy musanga tree that he had climbed for refuge began to sway. Beneath him, the men were hacking away at its trunk. As the tree fell, one of them tossed a cloth over the gorilla's head while another grabbed his arms and legs and tied them together.

"Ngyulla," the Africans told the white man in the Panama hat He was paying them to lead him through their forests to find go-rillas. Some hunts went on for days, so they were pleased that this gorilla had been so easy to find and capture. Although his cries had reached them from a wild berry patch, they might just as eas-ily have come from one of their corn or pineapple fields. So the Africans felt no qualms about killing the mother to take the son captive. Gorillas were plentiful in the Gabon forests in 1859. And they were no friend of the farmers. As far as the Africans were concerned, "Ngyulla is better off dead."

The white man, a twenty-four-year-old American, Paul Belloni du Chaillu, was delighted to have caught a live gorilla. He ad-mired the way this youngster tried to free himself from a forked stick they had clamped around his neck, and the way he continued to struggle even after his captors had bundled him into a canoe and paddled with him down one of the tributaries of the Congo River to the large clearing where du Chaillu had set up camp.

The small animal kept on biting and fighting as they dragged him out onto dry land and into the jerry-built village that du Chaillu had patriotically named Washington. Delighted with his spirited captive, the young man dubbed him Fighting Joe.

And Joe is, without a doubt, the first gorilla to have an English name. He is also the first whose story, although a short one, of life among human beings is a part of scientific record.

Joe never stopped struggling. He was quite young when he was captured and looked more like a small human being than he would have had he lived to maturity. So du Chaillu treated him as he might have treated a human child, an unlucky child, for it seems that the young explorer, who remained a bachelor all his life, would not have made an understanding father.

He described Joe as three-and-a-half feet tall and about three years old. How he arrived at that age is a mystery, and probably wrong. At that height, Joe would have been older. He seemed to be a healthy male specimen of lowland gorilla. And like most lowland gorillas, he was black except for a reddish sheen in the fur that grew like a cap on the top of his head. He also had short iron gray fur growing along his back and gradually blending into the long black hairs of his arms. This silvering fur, as well as his height, proves that he was beginning to mature.

Du Chaillu noted that Joe's black skin extended to the palms of his hands and the soles of his feet. He described Joe's eyes as "sunken" and decorated with eyebrows and lashes. He also mentioned Joe's "mustache" and "whiskers," all part of the "morose" expression that never left his face. Du Chaillu was describing a man-ape, not an animal, and this was a major shortcoming of his work. He clearly believed that he had captured some kind of miniature monster.

Besides that, du Chaillu discovered what he considered poor character traits in the young animal. First of all, he felt that Joe was ungrateful. The ill-tempered little rascal, as du Chaillu called him, was ungrateful to him for having spared his life. He was equally ungrateful to the Africans who cooked meats for him that he stubbornly refused to eat. Instead, the small gorilla would eat only vines and berries that the villagers gathered from the clearing in which they had captured him.

Worse still, Joe was treacherous. When his captor went to the great bother of building a strong bamboo cage for Joe's own protection, the animal deliberately gnawed through the bars and escaped.

The first time Joe slipped away, du Chaillu and the villagers searched all over Washington for him. Finally, after scouring the trees and the river too, du Chaillu returned to search his own hut. When he peered under his folding camp bed, he found himself staring into the "mean" eyes of the escapee.

After Joe had been forced back into his cage, he had to live with the forked stick fastened permanently around his neck. And when he retreated to the rear of that cage at du Chaillu's approach, the explorer interpreted Joe's fear as a deliberate snub and decided to teach him a lesson—no food at all for twenty-four hours.

After a few weeks, Joe would occasionally eat out of du Chaillu's hand. But he always retreated to the corner of his cage whenever one of the villagers came in. Du Chaillu believed that Joe remembered that it had been Africans who actually captured him. More likely Joe had learned to fear black people in some earlier experience in the forest.

Du Chaillu tried to tame Joe, as he would a dog. Yet at the same time he expected more from the small gorilla than he would ever have expected from a household pet. He wanted to meet Joe as an equal, and he wanted Joe to respond to him by offering his friendship.

The last time Joe escaped, he was already worn out from hunger and loneliness. When he finally reached the tall trees that surrounded Washington village, he was too weak to climb. This time it was easy for the Africans. All they did was drop a net over him and bring him back. Even then, absolutely exhausted, Joe kept fighting. It took several men one hour just to secure a metal collar around his neck. Now he was chained all the time.

Not totally without compassion, du Chaillu tossed a barrelful of hay into Joe's cage. Whenever he was tired, Joe would shake the hay and make himself a nest. At night, he would save some straw and put it on top of himself like a blanket. Those last nights, Joe moaned constantly in his sleep. Du Chaillu believed he was yearning for his mother. Ten days after the last escape, Joe died.

Paul du Chaillu is a puzzling personality. We know about his adventures because he loved publicity and wrote many travel books. But after a few books, he began to contradict himself, so it is hard to ferret out the truth.

He claimed he was born in Gabon, a west African area that still boasts a large gorilla population, where he lived in a coastal fort with his father, a French businessman. He never went to school but spent his childhood picking up African languages as well as a great deal of information about customs and legends from the peoples he befriended. He was especially fascinated by the tales they told about strange animals that lived in the as yet unmapped forests of central Africa.

After he was orphaned at seventeen, Paul du Chaillu sailed to the United States, to New Orleans, where people still spoke French. Living on the sales of a large collection of African plants he had brought with him, du Chaillu gradually made his way eastward to Philadelphia, New York, and Boston where he became a naturalized American in 1853.

Du Chaillu did not find it difficult to interest American geographers and naturalists in the idea of sending him back to Africa. Americans then were especially competitive with the British. And the presence of explorers such as the famous Scotsman, Dr. David Livingstone, who was in Africa searching for the source of the Nile River, tempted them to send this very attractive new American as their representative to what was then called the Dark Continent.

Zoologists in the 1850s were excitedly adding new animals to their lists. Du Chaillu knew how to play on their curiosity. He intrigued members of the Boston and Philadelphia Academies of Science with the promise of exotic specimens of animals and plants which he knew about from his African friends.

He assured the American scientists that he could bring them examples of these strange animals, especially one of the newly listed apes, the gorilla. He hoped to bring one back alive. But if he could not, he was equipped with the finest instruments for bringing them back dead.

Paul du Chaillu was typical of nineteenth-century explorers. He thought of himself as a man of many talents: part geographer, part journalist, and part scientist. Even as a scientist, du Chaillu wore several hats. En route to Africa, he stopped off in London and met with members of both the Royal Geographical Society and the Royal Astronomical Society. Both gave him tips on gathering scientific data. He added their instructions on mapping the African interior to his plans to collect plants and animals in his role as botanist and zoologist.

Perhaps the greatest change in science during the last century is that today's scientists know one discipline. Even within that they specialize, so that zoologists often study just one kind of animal, such as primates, and are then called *primatologists*. Today, most scientists know a great deal more about a narrower area than people did in the past.

But Paul du Chaillu lived in the heyday of the generalist. The three-masted ship which he sailed from England to west Africa was loaded with the paraphernalia of all his separate interests. This meant literally hundreds of boxes and cartons and sacks of equipment.

Du Chaillu regarded equatorial Africa as inhospitable to white men. He had no intentions of eating or dressing or traveling like a native. On the contrary, he brought along three straw hats, including the one he was wearing on the day he took Joe. He also brought seventy-two pairs of boots, twenty-four pairs of shoes, and twelve pairs of leather leggings to protect his legs from thorns and briars. His only concession to the jungle was a decision not to bother with the celluloid collars then fashionable in men's shirts.

But that was just the beginning. He carried six sextants and compasses for his astronomical charting, as well as five custom-made watches. And along with the watches came forty-eight specially made keys to wind them up, plus 100 feet of tape to measure trees.

He hired 100 men to carry these supplies, so his journey into the forests was certainly not a secret. Although he did not travel light, he packed skillfully. The wooden crates that arrived in Africa filled with 100 pounds each of laundry soap and arsenic, returned filled with plant and animal specimens. He had used up the soap and arsenic curing the animal skins. Du Chaillu was expert in taxidermy, the new art of stuffing and preserving animal specimens. Without preserved specimens, zoologists could not have studied new life-forms, because in the days before jet planes, freezers, and climate control, neither live or dead animals could last through a long trip.

The first efforts at preservation were sad. Poor marksmen killed too many animals with so many bullets that nothing was left to stuff. Others killed their specimens neatly enough, but then let them dry out so that before they ever reached a museum, the specimens had rotted or had been devoured by insects.

Du Chaillu was lucky. The only good manual on taxidermy in print before the twentieth century was written in French. Paul du Chaillu must have studied it. Without a doubt, he was one of the best animal preservers of his day.

Before Joe's body had grown cold, du Chaillu had made an incision in his back and cut a line straight through the thickest part of Joe's fur. Later, when he had stuffed the skin, no seam would show in the thick hair. Next, moving carefully outward from this cut, he removed all of Joe's skin. As he did so, he probably noticed that unlike humans, gorillas have no layer of fat between their skin and flesh.

Although gorillas seem very hairy compared to us, their pelage is not thick. It does grow long on most parts of the body. On the back it is short, full, and coarse, and grows diagonally away from the spine, not towards it as in humans. But the belly hair is fine and woolly.

Du Chaillu had learned a good deal about gorilla anatomy. He had already preserved Joe's mother and a great silverback male that he managed to kill neatly with just one shot.

After he had carefully peeled the skin in one piece, he prepared a mixture of arsenic and soap that taxidermists call *arsenic-soap,* over an open fire. He began by filling an iron caldron with equal parts of each ingredient, added a pinch of alum, sprinkled in some potash, and then stirred the mixture until it had boiled down to something that looked like molasses. This went into a wooden mold to cool. When it reached the consistency of butter, he brushed it over the whole skin. The poison stopped insects from getting at the skin, while at the same time it preserved the real color of the fur.

After he had carefully separated the flesh from the bones, he gave Joe's skeleton the same care. With one of his ten knives, hewn razor-sharp, he removed each bone. He had to label them carefully and keep them in the right order, like a puzzle that must not fall apart. Together, the bones of Joe, his mother, and the silverback gave du Chaillu the whole picture of gorilla structure.

The three skeletons lined up together made the differences clear. The adult male is almost twice as tall as the female. This is called *sexual dimorphism.* It occurs in many species, but it does not occur in the gorilla's closest relatives—*Homo sapiens.*

Another difference between the adult male, and the female and young gorilla, is the development of the thick bony ridges on top of the male's large skull. The ridge crossing from front to back is called the *sagittal crest*; the smaller one, crossing it at a right angle, is the *nuchal ridge.* They make the adult male look as if he is wearing a helmet. The ridges anchor the great muscles in the gorilla's jaw so that he can chew the thick bamboo and cane shoots that make up so much of his diet. Females and younger males also develop these crests, but to a much smaller degree.

The skeletons show arms longer than human arms, and legs much shorter in proportion to their bodies than ours. Gorillas have more ribs than humans. They don't have ankles, and they rarely walk upright on two legs.

The gorilla's skull is like our own, and the brain inside has all the same parts as a human brain. It is the same size as a human's at birth, but the gorilla brain stays that size, while the human brain continues to grow.

When du Chaillu sliced open Joe's stomach, he saw that like the animal's mother's, it contained vegetable matter—proof of what has subsequently been confirmed, that gorillas do not eat meat. He may also have noted that a gorilla's colon and cecum, parts of the intestines, are larger than a human's because the animal has to digest so much tough and fibrous material.

Du Chaillu set the bones and innards aside, and moved on to preserving the eyes: the supreme test of a skilled taxidermist. A gorilla's eyes, like human eyes, work together binocularly. They see in depth and in color, an adaptation that enables forest-dwelling animals to spot food, as well as danger, amidst the foliage.

Next came the ears. A gorilla's ears are small and set close to the head. They probably have the same power as a human ear that has not been dulled by listening to loud traffic, loud airplanes, or loud music. Only the nose, snoutlike and broader than that of the other apes, looks very different. But it probably has about the same power to smell as the other apes and humans.

As he finished, du Chaillu preserved Joe's hands and feet. The small hands looked silky and black, like elegant gloves that were very wrinkled, even in the young ape. Alive, Joe had grasped things with his palms downward, not upward as we do. On the backs of his hands he had fatty pads near the knuckles. These knuckle pads, in both chimpanzees and gorillas, protect their hands as they walk along four-leggedly in a "knuckle-walk." Joe's feet look like a second set of hands because the big toes are like thumbs that the gorilla uses to grasp tree limbs as he climbs.

"Fighting Joe" arrived in New York City in 1860, a beautifully stuffed animal with shiny black fur, except for a circle around the neck that had been stripped bare by the metal chain. Du Chaillu took his specimens with him to London, where he sold the enormous stuffed silverback to the British Museum for 566 pounds sterling, a fortune in those days.

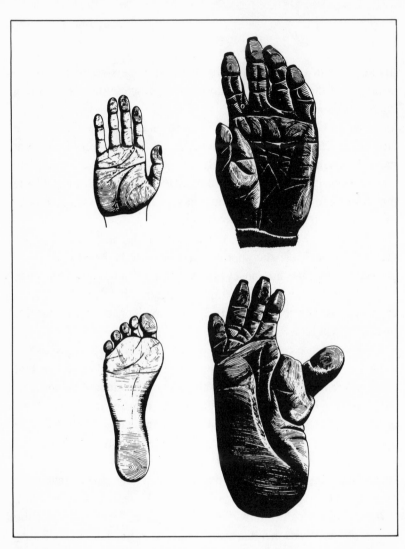

A human hand (top left) *compared with a gorilla hand. A human foot* (bottom left) *and a gorilla foot.* (Adapted from original drawing by J. Biegert as reproduced in *The Apes* by Vernon Reynolds, New York: E. P. Dutton, 1967)

From the moment du Chaillu appeared with his gorillas on the stage at the British Geographical Society, scientific pandemonium broke out. He was hailed by some as a great zoologist and explorer, and condemned by others as a fake. Friends pointed in pride to Joe and to du Chaillu's maps of equatorial Africa. But enemies noted errors and inconsistencies in the book he had published, and called his accounts exaggerations, if not outright lies.

They laughed at his explanation that he had "borrowed" pictures from the British Museum files because his own photographs had been destroyed by rampaging tribesmen revenging themselves

Paul du Chaillu on his triumphant return from Africa (Royal Geographical Society, London)

The frontispiece from du Chaillu's best-selling travel book in 1861

for the accidental gunshot killing of a Pygmy child. They rejected his explanation of why the writing style was not his own: As a native French-speaking person, he had hired an American journalist to check his English grammar. The journalist had unwittingly taken liberties with the text.

But the book sold well. Its profits helped him return to Africa in 1866 to bring back more gorillas. From then on, until he died almost forty years later in St. Petersburg, Russia, du Chaillu traveled the world and wrote about his adventures. When he died in 1903, the British newspapers mourned him as a great man. By then his maps had proved excellent. But he was hailed above all for introducing the gorilla to the West.

Yet people still condemn him today, accusing him of making himself a hero at the gorilla's expense. They blame Paul du Chaillu for turning the gorilla into a monster. Unfairly. Du Chaillu may have embellished his adventures, but he did not create the myths. They had been made first by the Africans who had beguiled him with gorilla tales.

Conservationists today criticize du Chaillu for using his gun. But he was doing only what was scientifically sound in a day when naturalists collected specimens for zoologists. Few scientists were then ready to study the lives of living gorillas. They dismissed the bulk of du Chaillu's field observations of a gorilla group as sheer fantasy.

Du Chaillu's language is old-fashioned and loaded with words such as *king* and *queen* that apply to human society, not to the animal world. But what he saw has been documented again by modern observers.

Paul du Chaillu's treatment of Joe could have been worse. He did keep the young ape alive for a while, and he did keep an honest record of the experience. If he misread Joe as a half-human demon rather than an innocent young animal, that was a blind spot of the time in which he lived. We cannot blame him for that.

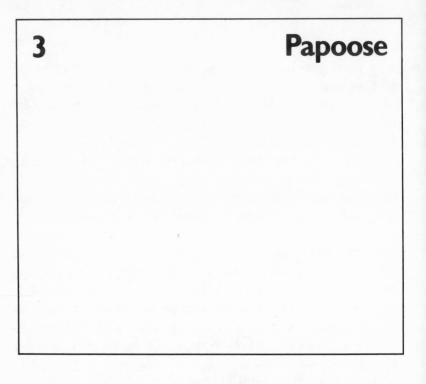

3   Papoose

The hair on the silverback's shoulders had begun to thin, but little Papoose did not seem to care that he had aged. She had been close to him all of her life, surrounded by the rest of the gorilla group. No one knows who her mother was. But at the time the primatologist first observed her in 1967, she was about eighteen months old and an orphan who had been adopted by Whinney, the group's ancient silverback leader.

Papoose had probably stopped nursing about six months earlier. Now she lived like the other mountain gorillas on a rich diet of vines, leaves, fruits, and fungi. Something peculiar to the vegetation in her part of the east African mountains had already blackened her teeth and her tongue. The same thing happens to all the other gorillas in Rwanda's Parc des Volcans, 10,000 feet above sea level near the equator.

Despite her black teeth and tongue, she still seems pretty to the modern scientists who have spent years watching her. They describe Papoose as a sweet little animal with gentle eyes. She is also an unusual animal because during the first six years of her life she was in one of the few gorilla groups in the entire world that is habituated to human beings. This means the animals will allow an observer to come within a yard of them without changing the way they behave.

When she was very small, Papoose used to wake up each morning in the bowl-shaped nest she shared with old Whinney. She would peer over its crude side at the eddies of white fog that whirled along the ground, obscuring the deep undergrowth that covers the earth in this thick forest on the mountainside.

Snug in the nest, she would watch the old silverback stretch his arms, then reach out and select some galium vines, or perhaps wild celery or thistle stems, for his breakfast. His hot breath would meet the cold air, leaving a puff of smoke wafting in the breeze. Then Papoose would copy him, as she would have copied her mother, and stuff some of the same food into her own mouth.

Soon they would climb out of the nest, abandoning it forever. And little Papoose, along with the rest of the group, would follow the silverback into the thick foliage.

Tunneling through vines and briars, Papoose would join the other gorillas in their morning's work of travel and feeding. Moving in single file, often hidden from each other by waist-high ground cover, the gorillas rumbled pleasure belches as they ate.

As a baby, Papoose had learned to recognize these happy sounds. She had also learned to know the sharp barks, or "pig grunts," that told her to behave, and the whoop bark that Whinney used as an alarm when he came upon something strange and unfamiliar.

Although she might be only a yard away from Whinney, the thick undergrowth kept the gorillas invisible from each other, as well as from the human observer who was tracking them. These social sounds—grunts, rumbles, and barks—hold the gorilla group together. The same husky barks and low rumbling tones, along with the pungent gorilla smell, keep the human observer on its trail. Observers know their animals intimately, deep in the mountain mists.

Papoose is among the last of a vanishing species—the mountain gorilla, *Gorilla gorilla beringei*. In 1903, when Germany had begun colonizing east Africa, a Captain Oscar von Beringe discovered what may then have been a population of several thousand mountain gorillas. They were living in small groups at high elevations scattered among the Virunga Mountains. Since that time the wild populations have dwindled drastically, and there may be only a few hundred gorillas left in the area.

It is ironic that the lives of this remnant group are so much more familiar to scientists than the ways of their more numerous lowland cousins, *Gorilla gorilla gorilla,* whose bodies, like Fighting Joe's, fill our museums, and whose living representatives fill our zoos. Scientists have stubbornly maintained research centers in protected parks in these unwelcoming mountains. Below, in the lowland forests, the gorillas are less protected by conservationists, and they run away from all humans, including peaceful scientific observers.

The idea of conserving gorillas in parks like our own national parks began in the 1920s, when the American Museum of Natural History sent Carl Akeley and his wife, Mary, to Africa to prepare a mountain gorilla exhibition. Akeley went to the town of Kigoma, in what was then the Belgian Congo, and explored the magnificent mountainside. He shot and preserved five specimens, ancestors of Papoose which are standing now behind glass at the New York museum. Then, after Akeley had killed the few animals he needed, he devoted the remaining years of his life to encouraging the Belgian government to set aside part of the mountains as a gorilla preserve. Akeley died there in 1926, and his wife buried him on the saddle of the mountain in the Kabara meadow. Three years later the Albert National Park was enlarged to include the entire chain of Virunga volcanoes. In 1932 the area became a gorilla sanctuary. Without it, none of these gorillas might be alive today.

From 1932 until 1959, the mountain gorillas lived private lives. Then George B. Schaller, an American ethologist who was interested in the great apes, took his wife, Kay, to the Kabara meadow. There they spent a year, wandering among the trees, following, watching, and recording gorilla lives. Schaller's observations led to *The Year of the Gorilla,* a vivid description of the gorilla's slow, peaceful ways.

Schaller's work changed everything. He had proved that a scientist could travel, unarmed, through the remote mountains and observe the animals. Before him, most primatologists had restricted their fieldwork to smaller apes and monkeys. Field primatology or ethology, in which the scientist sits patiently in the forest, blending in with the scenery, had only begun. The rules had not been worked out, and no one knew how far up the evolutionary ladder they could go. Monkeys seemed difficult enough to observe accurately.

But at the same time that Schaller set out for the Virunga volcanoes, another science-shaking study was beginning 200 miles south in Tanzania. There an Englishwoman had begun observing wild chimpanzees at the Gombe Stream on Lake Tanganyika. Jane Goodall's work began in the hope of finding some connection between the lives of the apes and the lives of early man. It took Goodall almost a year to begin habituating the chimpanzees. And since gorillas seemed shyer, it looked as if someone even more patient, if possible, would have to habituate gorillas. The promise of what this could reveal was alluring. Schaller's success indicated that unprovoked, gorillas are harmless.

The scientist who had the patience and courage to continue where Schaller had left off was another American, Dian Fossey. She arrived in Africa in 1966. Except for some months spent studying animal behavior at Cambridge University in England, she has lived there ever since.

Fossey established the Karisoke Research Center in Rwanda, at Ruhengeri, 200 kilometers from the capital and 1,000 feet above Lake Kivu on the slope of Mount Visoke. Except for a few African trackers, she spent her first years alone, identifying gorilla groups and habituating the gorillas so that she was able to move among them undisturbed.

Her early years were trial and error. She had read Schaller's work and had met Goodall. But soon she developed her own approach. Moving into the forest, she belched the deep belly-rumble of a happily eating animal. Soon she was accepted by Whinney and Papoose's group.

Eventually she wanted to know how many other groups and how many animals were left in the mountains. She needed to map the range and take a census. But this was too great a task to do alone. With help from universities and foundations, scientists who were students of animal behavior, botany, and parasitology joined her at the Karisoke Research Center.

One of the first to arrive in the fall of 1972 was Alexander H. (Sandy) Harcourt, an Englishman. Two years later he was joined by Kelly Stewart, an American. A botanist from Missouri joined the center briefly in 1975, and a Rwandese from Ruhengeri came in 1976.

The camp is small, and only a few people can live there at a time. Between 1971 and 1975, nine students helped explore the six dormant volcanoes where the gorillas live. They quite literally counted noses. They sketched, photographed, and identified each animal by the distinct markings: indentations on the bridge of its

Kelly Stewart and Sandy Harcourt (Bettyann Kevles)

nose and the shape of its nostrils, which Fossey calls a *nose-print*. As unique in mountain gorillas as a human's fingerprints, nose-prints help the different census takers identify new animals and ensure that they do not count the same ones twice.

First Fossey, and then Harcourt and Stewart, became part of Papoose's world. Following Whinney's lead, Papoose never feared them. The humans always approached her slowly, crouching or on their knees, and they never threatened her by standing taller than a gorilla or looking directly into her eyes.

Sometimes, if Papoose sat scratching away the dry skin around her thighs, the observer would scratch a make-believe itch. And when Papoose plucked a blackberry or broke off a wild bamboo stalk to munch, the human did the same and belched the same happy sounds so that Papoose knew no harm was meant.

Papoose's days followed the same pattern throughout the tropical year, for the seasons resemble each other near the equator. Even the rainfall at this height is fairly constant, varying from heavy to very heavy. Nighttime is cold, especially at 13,000 feet, where frost forms rapidly when the temperature drops below freezing. Mountain gorillas have especially thick fur that helps protect them from the chill.

Papoose's family in Rwanda has even longer hair than other groups of mountain gorillas that live several thousand feet lower down the mountain range in the Kahuzi-Biega National Park in adjacent Zaire. But thick fur is not always enough, and pneumonia is one of the greatest natural threats to gorilla health everywhere in the Virungas.

Traveling and feeding in the morning might take Papoose's group anywhere within the four or five square kilometers that make up its range. Within these boundaries old Whinney knew the terrain well. One day he might lead Papoose and the others in a follow-the-leader sprint across icy streams, carefully balancing on stepping-stones or a fallen tree because these gorillas seem to hate to get their feet wet. Or he could take them through thick nettle patches which gorillas, with their thick skins, do not seem to feel.

By midday the sun has usually burnt off the gray morning mist, leaving the high meadows aglow with color. Relatives of North American flowers bloom amid the high grass: daisy-yellows and daisy-whites, as well as exotic orchids, red and purple against the glistening forest greens.

Midday is rest time for the adult gorillas. But it is playtime for the youngsters, who play together more than any other young ape. They frolic, wrestling and tumbling about on the ground. Gorillas also love to swing and slide from the high tree limbs, and the littlest ones use the silverback's sloped body as a slide. They also play alone, picking leaves and flowers or doing acrobatics in the foliage.

The mother gorillas cluster close to the silverback at rest times. They seem to know that their infants want to play with each other. And they also know that when their infants play, they get a chance to sleep. The silverback acts as a "day-care center"; he is alert if a small animal gets in trouble. He, too, may try to doze. But if Papoose rolls into him as she prances around his crude day nest, he may reprimand her gently with a quiet grunt, or twit her nose with a fresh-picked daisy. And then she chuckles, for gorillas seem to express pleasure with a low laugh or a giggle.

If the sun is bright, the adults take a long rest. Trapped by nature in a wet habitat, they adore the sun and flop back to enjoy it when they can.

Eventually, the silverback must move. His own body, no less than 350 pounds, needs sustenance. Scientists estimate that male gorillas eat at least 60 pounds of food every day. The smaller females and infants are also hungry, so the silverback leads them on another feeding journey later in the afternoon.

Gorillas spend a great part of their lives eating. After they have found what they are looking for, they sit down on the ground and pull lots of the vines or leaves together. When it is all gathered, they peel the outer stems off the tougher stalks and eat the insides.

The lush vegetation also gives them water. Scarcely a soul has seen a gorilla drink out of the many cool streams that gurgle through the mountain gullies. But some have spotted gorillas bending down to the cupped surfaces of leaves, sucking up the little pools of moisture.

Papoose's home range is very steep. And depending on where she happens to be on the mountainside, she looks for different plants. The silverback seems able to remember from year to year exactly where and when a special treat, like the blackberries that grow on the ridges, will be ripe. Or when the pygeum, a tree that looks like an oak, will bear its bitter almond-shaped fruits.

A small part of Papoose's range is grassland dotted with giant hagenia trees. The gorillas scoot across the open meadow, apparently unhappy when they are so exposed to view, and rush to the safety of the trees. Hagenia trunks are occasionally six feet in diameter, their branches growing low and broad with curtains of moss closing off secret niches among the leaves. These trees are like villages for the gorillas. The smaller animals build nests in them, swing in the moss, and eat the ferns that grow thick on the tree trunks.

Sometimes the silverback leads the group up high, where the ground cover thins and an occasional buffalo or elephant grazes. But it seems he moves up there only when he wants special food. In general, gorillas prefer the lush, dense vegetation on the lower slopes.

Papoose spent her infancy and girlhood frolicking with the other gorillas. As she matured, she spent lots of time with a special friend, Petula, who is about four years older than she is. Perhaps they sought each other out because Papoose missed having a mother. Or perhaps there was a different reason. But they were clearly friends, and this is rare among adult female gorillas. So the observers watched them closely.

Papoose also played frequently with a young silverback whom Fossey named Uncle Bert. Then, when old Whinney died, Uncle Bert replaced him as the leader of the group. Papoose stayed in the group and followed Uncle Bert just as she had followed old Whinney, who probably was Uncle Bert's father. But one day in 1974, Papoose left her group, and her behavior revealed a whole new side of gorilla society.

All the observers had noticed the stranger, a new silverback in the forest who was hanging around the group. They called him Nunki. A few days after Papoose met him, she left Uncle Bert to join Nunki. But she did not leave alone. Her old friend Petula, who had played with her when she was a youngster, also left, abandoning her four-year-old son, Augustus. He stayed behind with Uncle Bert.

But Uncle Bert was unwilling to let two of his females just go off. When their paths crossed in the forest, he confronted Nunki with the two females.

Both giant males stood upright, their huge bare chests dwarfing their shorter legs. Uncle Bert opened his mouth and began a series of hooting sounds that built up louder and louder until they culminated in a barrel-like beat when he opened his great hands and pounded against his chest. *Pok, pok, pok:* a hollow sound like the rolling of muffled drums. Then Nunki beat his chest too, and pounded the ground, returning the call.

Uncle Bert retaliated. He yanked at the nearby foliage and, dragging a giant branch, ran through the forest. Both silverbacks broke off more chunks of trees and charged. The ground grew thick with forest debris, yet the silverbacks had not touched each other.

Then the charade ended. No more parallel displays of strength or thumpings on the ground. Now the two animals raged toward each other, met, and grappled. They attacked with open mouths, biting savagely on faces and limbs. The hair on their shoulders stood on end. The flesh below their eyebrows moved back and forth in frenzy.

In the background, the younger males and females backed away to watch the battle from the cover of the trees, to hear the *pok pok* of the chest beats and the snarling cries.

Like prizefighters, the huge silverbacks swayed, interlocked. At least 10 meters away, safe in a distant tree, an observer watched through binoculars.

The undergrowth half hid the fray, but the harsh barks echoed through the air. And the gray bodies, tangled in a heap, released a stench of fear from hard-worked sweat glands. The smell filled the forest.

At last they stopped. Both were wounded but still very much alive.

Other fights between silverbacks may have ended with an innocent victim left in its wake. Twice an observer found the corpses of infants but did not actually see them killed. According to Fossey, the battling silverbacks seem to go deliberately for the infants, as if they wanted to destroy not just the enemy but all of his descendants. Harcourt and Stewart are not sure, and consider the infants' deaths still unexplained.

This fight, however, left no victims. Uncle Bert retreated, without the runaways. He seemed the loser. Yet within three days, Papoose returned to Uncle Bert. A week passed, and Petula, too, left Nunki and headed for the high grasslands where she could move quickly. She raced on alone until she found Uncle Bert and rejoined her old group. There Petula ignored little Augustus and left immediately with her old friend, Papoose, to join still a third suitor, a handsome silverback the observer called Samson.

The three gorillas—Samson, Petula, and Papoose—stayed together for a month. Then Nunki reappeared.

Nunki was still alone when Papoose and Petula finally made up their minds to stay with him. Over the next two years, Nunki attracted three more females, and during that time both Papoose and Petula gave birth to Nunki's babies. With a new generation begun, Nunki's new group seems well established. And an observer has been able to document the ups and downs of a young silverback as he established a foothold in the forest.

Papoose cannot be accused of being unfaithful to Uncle Bert. She had grown up with him, and she treated him like a brother. There seems to be growing evidence that in the wild, animals which are very familiar with each other as youngsters do not breed together when they are grown. Even human primates raised together in communes, such as in an Israeli kibbutz, seem to marry individuals from outside.

Papoose's emigration to another group appears to be the way

gorilla groups change and grow. Most primate families are held together by bonds between mothers and their daughters. It is the males who grow up and leave home. Only among Africa's chimpanzees and gorillas does the female also move on.

The silverback unites his group while the females merely tolerate each other. They are strangers, brought together by convenience, so that their infants can have playmates and the great male can protect them all.

In Uncle Bert's group, Augustus was left, for all practical purposes, an orphan, just as Papoose had been seven years earlier. Had either of them been a small chimpanzee, they might have died. But luckily the silverback really cares for young gorillas, and Augustus was happy with Uncle Bert.

4   Harcourt and Stewart with the Mountain Gorillas

In October 1972, it was raining in England when Sandy Harcourt took the plane at Heathrow Airport. It was also raining when he landed in Ruhengeri three days later. Another academic year was starting, and Harcourt was returning to his studies—but not at Cambridge where he had already earned a degree in zoology. This time he was headed into the field.

The Virunga Mountains were new to him, but this was not his first visit to Africa. He had been born 500 miles to the east in Kenya, which he had left with his family in 1955. Slim, pale and quiet, Harcourt drove through the crowded market towns along the shores of Lake Kivu in a four-wheel-drive car. Then he began winding his way up the mountain. At 8,000 feet the road ended, and he got out. He carried what he could and, with African bearers, continued on foot up the red dirt trail that wound another 2,000 feet to the saddle area between the peaks.

Only a few corrugated iron cabins sat there in the high grass. A stream flowed by, and a wood fire burned red in a pit in front of the cabins, defying the constant dampness. The colors were vivid.

The rains kept a myriad of greens deep-hued and never sun-bleached.

Fossey showed Harcourt to the cabin, a small square with straw matting on the floor, that would be his for the next few years. With Fossey's dog, Cindy, he explored the camp to learn the center's procedures and the problems of gorilla watching.

In 1972, the 17,000 hectares of the park suffered daily intrusions from neighboring tribes. The park rangers did not patrol it well then, and Watusi cattle herders, who had once been nomads from the north, now brought their herds inside to graze, destroying the vegetation the gorillas lived on.

They were not the only outlaws. Poachers trapped antelope and sometimes accidentally trapped and killed gorillas. Woodcutters and honey gatherers destroyed the trees, and some hunters killed the gorillas to use various parts of their bodies in magical potions. So the researchers had to police the 17,000 hectares of the park, along with their scientific work.

The scientists first described the gorillas' behavior when they were under siege. Then later, after the Rwandese improved the patrols, the scientists were able to compare the ways the animals lived in a more relaxed atmosphere. With the dangers lessened, Harcourt noted, the gorillas spread out, extending their range. This suggests that the structure of each group is dependent on more than the silverback's personal appeal. It is apparently affected by the living conditions in the whole area.

Fossey showed Harcourt all around the camp that day. Even as he listened to her, beyond the horizon in the forests, the gorillas munched and slept, unaware that they were about to meet a new human observer.

Harcourt could begin his work immediately because Fossey had already habituated the gorilla groups. Instead of having to let the animals gradually get used to him, he was "introduced" by Fossey and shown how to gain acceptance by the silverback whose personality dominates each group.

Harcourt began his work familiar with all that Schaller and Fossey had revealed about the general shape of gorilla life. So he could begin at once with a more specific goal. Gorillas, he knew, are the only apes that live in close-knit groups. He wanted to discover the social forces that held these groups together.

He met Uncle Bert's family first. Papoose was still small then, and Petula the mother of a two-year-old-son, Augustus. For a year he tried to observe them every day, recording in painstaking detail the way each animal got along with the others.

A second year passed, and another scientist joined the small research community on the side of Mount Visoke. Kelly Stewart had just received a degree in anthropology from Stanford University in California, and had enrolled in the subdepartment of animal behavior at Madingley, Cambridge, England, where Harcourt was working on a doctorate.

Like Harcourt, Stewart was accepted quickly by Uncle Bert and then by the rest of his group. And like Harcourt, she had a special focus to her research. While he tried to understand the relations between adult gorillas, she looked at the females and infants to see how their friendships with each other, and with the silverbacks, affected the changes within the groups.

The years since the beginning of Schaller's project have been crucial to the science of ethology. It has grown from dependence on a single naturalist's sharp insights to a precise science. Harcourt and Stewart use new methods in their work. They feed their observations into a computer to arrive at as true a picture as possible of gorilla society.

The young ethologists began each forest day in much the same way. Rising at dawn, just like the gorillas that they were watching, they breakfasted quickly in camp. Then in Swahili, the international language of east Africa, they asked their African trackers to help them find the gorillas. They dressed warmly and stuffed their haversacks with raincoats, binoculars, stopwatches, pencils, papers, and sandwiches. They packed their visas, too. For although gorillas can cross the border into the neighboring country of Zaire quite freely, humans need proper credentials. They would leave together but separate soon. Each observer watched alone.

Pale skins in green denims, the scientists left camp booted and gloved—protecting everything but their faces from the stinging nettles and tangled briars they would push through below, and the occasional hailstorm that would pelt them from above.

Nettles, especially, were a constant threat, as were the slippery paths that turn to mud in the heavy rains. There were days when the observer could hear the gorilla's low chuckles above the buzz of insects and the shrill touraco's cry, and smell the pungent gorilla smell. But the undergrowth would be so thick that he could not see them.

On those days, he settled for examining the animal's spoor, its dung. It tells a great deal about the animal's health and eating habits. Fossey actually uncovered the only known instance of gorilla cannibalism when she found tiny bones and fur in the dung of a female shortly after a small infant had disappeared.

On good days, the researcher quickly finds the nesting site that the gorillas have left earlier that morning. From the number of nests and the way they are clustered, the scientist knows exactly which of the nine groups that roam the study area had been there the night before.

The trail begins with these freshly abandoned nests. The scientist picks it up, following the crushed leaves and broken celery stalks that the gorillas leave as they move along. More dung and more devastated vegetation make a clear trail to the trained eye.

But sometimes a hazardous one. The gorillas move alongside steep canyons, and sometimes they too slip and fall. Fossey has found gorilla bones lying in the bottom of ravines. On a good day, however, the scientist moves along swiftly until he hears the familiar pig-grunts and catches a whiff of gorilla.

Occasionally Harcourt or Stewart would meet the gorillas while the animals were traveling and feeding. They noted that it is during these periods, not when the group is resting, that gorillas mate. The gorilla couple, hidden from the rest of their group by the dense vegetation, apparently needs the privacy. When the gorillas allow humans close enough to watch them mate, this is especially significant because it shows that the animals have accepted the human observers into their world.

Schaller saw very little sexual activity during his year in the wild, and Fossey did not see much more. Although the gorillas seemed to accept human observers easily, they did not relax with them and behave normally in their presence for a long, long time.

Usually the scientists catch up with the gorilla group during its noon siesta. The adult animals, mothers and silverback, try to sleep. But this is when the youngsters play. Later, when the adults wake up, are the the crucial hours in a gorilla's life. It is the time when all of the animals mix socially. And it is when the scientists record the subtle relationships among them, the gentle nods and shoves that show each animal's very special place in the group's hierarchy, a forecast of its future in the forest.

These are an ethologist's best working hours. The scientist may sit several yards away. Occasionally the undergrowth is so thick that he has to climb a tree to see. Then the observer takes out his binoculars to watch. But often the observer is able to crawl to within just a few feet of the animals. The only tools he needs are a stopwatch, a pencil, and paper.

Fossey insists that the African guides quit the scene before the gorillas see them. She is adamant, afraid to allow the gorillas to get used to any Africans for fear that if something should happen and the research center shut down, gorillas habituated to her African trackers would be unable to defend themselves against other African hunters and poachers.

Uncle Bert accepted the observers pretty easily after a while. But when ancient Whinney died and he took over, he was very wary. Years passed before he seemed relaxed with his human companions. The observer is still careful not to disturb him. When the scientist moves, he knuckle-walks, imitating Uncle Bert. And when he finds a good vantage point, he sits or kneels or crouches as he writes.

Harcourt takes a check sheet from the haversack. All his check sheets are the same, but they differ from Stewart's and from any other observer's. They are tailor-made for this particular study.

						IN	
	VOC	ACT	AP 5	AP 2	CONT	SG	LV 2
1							
2							
3							
4							
5							
6							
7							
8							
9							
10							
11							
12							
13							
14							
15							

Harcourt's check sheet has columns for specific behaviors such as VOCalizing, ACTivity, who APproaches whom within 5 meters and within 2 meters, and who CONTacts whom and in what way—for example, patting, grooming, or leaning against each other. The boxes running down the sheet at left are for 1-minute time intervals.

In the IN and OUT boxes (top center), Harcourt records which animals are in or out of his sight in three 5-minute intervals. In the shaded

Harcourt's look like graph paper, with the top boxes describing kinds of behavior and the side boxes listing 1-minute intervals. With the help of a stopwatch, he checks boxes every 60 seconds.

And he stays alert. After the long hike through tunnels of vines, he might be tired; and watching Uncle Bert stretched out, arms akimbo dozing in a patch of sunlight, is infectious. But he resists.

		OUT					
LV 5	Y	PTH					

boxes, he notes the date, page number of the check sheet, and the number of the gorilla group he is watching. The boxes immediately below them are for feeding information—for example, who feeds on what part of what plant species.

The wide spaces running down the sheet at the right are for Harcourt's miscellaneous comments, such as noting that the animals are disturbed by the sound of an airplane or by poachers.

Each slight movement is important, and a short doze might make him miss something.

Harcourt has seen Papoose edge toward Uncle Bert and turn her rump towards him, almost begging him to groom her. Gorillas do not groom each other's fur as often as most other primates. When they do, it is for reassurance. Uncle Bert is acting like an older brother when he pulls his fingers through Papoose's hair, removing dead skin and old leaves.

Sometimes one animal moves towards another to reach out and pat him, then moves on. This kind of brief, lethargic patting must mean something. Harcourt marks it down. When the check sheets are all filled in and tabulated a continent away, he is confident that the gestures will emerge into a pattern.

The check sheets are important, and so are maps that plot each animal's geographical position in the group. They are a way of recording how different members of a group get along together. Harcourt and Stewart have collected many different maps which they later analyzed and put together on graphs and charts, giving a visual idea of the gorillas' social relationships.

The maps record where the gorillas may have been seated throughout one whole rest period. Instead of plotting every sixty seconds, Harcourt marks these maps in quarter-hour intervals. First he may mark where each gorilla settled, made a crude day

Harcourt uses circle maps to record each animal's position in relation to a target individual. The rings reflect 5-meter intervals. In the box below the map, he records the individual's motion—Eating, Still, or moving about (Locomotion).

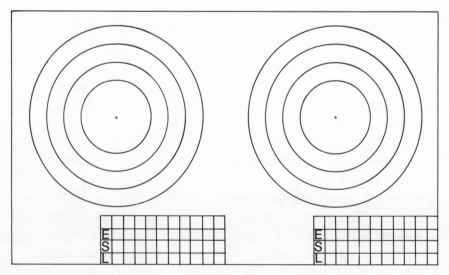

nest, and slept. Then he may record how the animals moved as the afternoon progressed.

All their data bring out a startling picture of what holds the group together. The silverback is the focus. Stewart's data show the different adult females—except for Papoose and Petula, whose friendship seems to be unique—not bothering with each other. When their babies are small, the mothers stay close to Uncle Bert. But as their children grow older, the mothers gradually move towards the edge of the group. By the time the infant is four, the mother sits on the fringes of the circle until a new baby arrives, bringing her back to the center, where she can feel protected, close to the silverback.

An angry "Wraagh" from a strange silverback, perhaps Nunki this time, and the group moves quickly toward Uncle Bert. Threatened, he stands upright with his teeth set in a determined grimace, and the females, infants, and blackbacks, or young males, cluster around him.

Mapping and checking, Harcourt and Stewart have analyzed the social bonds that hold a group together and the evolutionary forces that propel females like Papoose to leave. They are sure now that the silverback alone keeps his females together, and that only one or two of the young males will stay in the group, probably the oldest sons. The extra males will wander off when they are about eleven years old. They will drift through the forest alone until they are older and silvered; then they will attract their own females, as Nunki did.

The females will stay with Uncle Bert, the father of most of their infants. But the silverback's daughters, and sisters like Papoose, will migrate to another male. They will not just leave to wander about, but they will immediately join another group.

They will try to choose a silverback who can protect them and their babies. If they make a good choice, they transfer only once. But some females, like those whose babies have been killed in fights, transfer over and over again until they find a silverback who can protect them.

The females have moved so much that it is hard to trace a family tree. Harcourt and Stewart tried by matching the gorilla's features, especially the nose-prints. They would like to know the mothers, cousins, and aunts in the different groups. Among some of the animals the resemblance is startling, just as it is among humans.

When the siesta ends and the gorillas move on to another travel-feed, the observer usually starts back. Sometimes he or she is a two-hour hike from camp and must hurry. Sunsets are swift near the equator, and it is dangerous to be out alone in the forest after dark. The observers find their separate ways back.

There, in the orange lamplight, the pit fire a beacon, they heat their suppers over small paraffin stoves. One night in 1975, Stewart's stove caught fire while she was at the other side of the camp. Piles of check sheets, months of careful observations, and her cabin were reduced to ashes. Upset, she did not grieve but returned to the forest and started all over again.

After dinner, the scientists usually type their notes and compare the day's observations. They are looking at different angles of gorilla society, but they know that their separate studies can help each other and will produce a panoramic picture of gorilla life.

In June 1977, Dr. Harcourt married Kelly Stewart in London. They plan to return to Africa, to set up their own camp and take a census of another holdout of the great gorillas.

They know that they are up against overwhelming odds. The mountain gorillas may now be as few as 300 individuals. But they have little faith in zoos and believe that gorillas belong in their native rain forests. They are determined to fight to preserve these forests for the animals who live within them.

Science is important, but they are careful to point out that their research ends where the lives of the gorillas might be disturbed. Throughout their vigils, soaked by the constant rain, they always stopped observing if the gorillas seemed upset. Science is the tool they are using to bring about the conservation of a species— *Gorilla gorilla beringei*.

5 Snowflake

The rain forest of Nko in the lowlands of Río Muni has shrunk since Fighting Joe watched his mother die in nearby Gabon. There are more cultivated fields today, and lumber companies have cut roads across the rugged swamps. Yet what remains is much as it used to be. And wild gorillas still raid the farmers' fields. They destroy whole crops of bananas in hours by bending the stalks until they break, to eat their central piths.

So it happened that on the first day of October 1966, another gorilla mother lay dying from bullet wounds, an incriminating banana branch still in her hand. Benito Mané stood in the morning mist surveying his banana grove. He looked from the twisted banana plants to the dead animal, and then he noticed a small white creature clinging to her black fur.

"Nfumno ngi," he said, which means "white gorilla" in the language of the Fang people. And Nfumno remains the orphan's official name, although he is called *Copito de Nieve* in Spanish, the language of colonial Río Muni, and *Snowflake* in English.

But whichever name is used, each means the same. The gorilla

Snowflake just after his discovery in Río Muni (Jorge Sabater-Pi, National Geographic Society)

is an albino. By a genetic fluke, Snowflake inherited a rare inability to use a substance called *melanin* that lets the body's cells manufacture pigment. Snowflake has white fur, mostly white skin, and faintly blue pink eyes. Albinism is familiar among human beings, and it is not unknown in other animals. But Snowflake is the only white gorilla in memory.

Seventy years earlier, an American professor working in west Africa heard rumors about another white gorilla. But although he searched, he never found it. Gorillas with one white hand or foot have appeared from time to time, but these animals usually turned black all over as they grew up.

Among the traditions of the Fang tribe who live in what is now the Republic of Equatorial Guinea, there are many ape legends. One recalls an albino chimpanzee which the Fang revere as a totem (an animal considered related to the clan and used as its symbol). But the Fang have no legend of a white gorilla. So the farmer who discovered Snowflake treasured him. He brought the remarkable infant to his thatched hut, where he built him a cage and lined it deep with leaves, twigs, and vines from the forest. Then he fed Snowflake wild buds and fruits.

After four days, Benito Mané picked up the nineteen-and-a-half-pound two-year-old and carried him down the dusty road to the seaport of Bata. Once in the city, he went straight to Señor Jorge Sabater-Pi, director of the Ikunde Animal Acclimatization Center. And Señor Sabater-Pi bought Snowflake from him at once.

Sabater-Pi had lived in Spanish Guinea since 1945. He divided his time there between two jobs. He directed the Ikunde Center as an outpost of the Barcelona Zoo, a halfway house for animals on their way to zoos, and he went into the forest to study the wide range of animal life, especially primate life.

Señor Sabater-Pi is committed to preserving as much natural forest as possible. Yet he believes that it is only a matter of time before all of this land will be under cultivation. He feels that zoos are crucial for preserving rare animals, and that stations such as the one at Ikunde give the animals the best chance of surviving the shock of capture and adjustment to captivity.

Interested above all in evolution, Sabater-Pi was fascinated by the great apes, especially gorillas. Just a few months before Snowflake's appearance, Sabater-Pi, along with his American collaborators, Drs. Clyde Jones and Arthur Riopelle, who was then director of the Delta Regional Primate Facility in Louisiana, one of a string of seven primate laboratories sponsored by the U.S. government, had begun a survey of the ways gorillas fit into the ecology of the forest world. With time out to study Snowflake, their research continued for another two years. When in 1969 Río Muni became independent, the Ikunde Center closed and Sabater-Pi and his family returned to Spain.

Although the lowland gorillas have been known to science since 1847, they are still a mystery. No one even knows how many live in these forests. And no one has studied their behavior as closely as the scientists at Mount Visoke have analyzed the lives of mountain gorillas like Papoose.

The lowland gorillas have lived in fear of humans for generations. As they adapted to the forest, gorillas learned to include cultivated crops in their diet. Consequently, humans have hunted
them mercilessly for revenge, as well as for food or just for fun.

All we know with certainty is that the gorilla population is
dropping as swiftly as the human population expands. And as people clear more forest for fields or chop down trees for timber, the
gorillas are squeezed into smaller ranges. The lowland gorilla has
not even had the slight advantage that the mountain gorillas, who
have been protected since 1932 in nature preserves, have had.

When Jones and Sabater-Pi set out to track and observe Snowflake's relatives, they had a more difficult time finding them than
the scientists had finding mountain gorillas in the Virunga Mountains. The lowland rain forest is often impossible to cross, and
they had to hack their way through the undergrowth with knives.

But more frustrating than the terrain are the gorillas themselves.
Man is the predator they fear most. At the first hint of people, they
vanish. The scientists first had to find them.

They depended on skilled native guides, who managed to locate
gorilla groups by tracking them from their nests or by listening for
the sound of gorillas breaking branches as they built those nests.
The guides signaled the scientists, who set out wearing dark cloth-
ing to blend in with the foliage and kept their movements slow and
deliberate so they would not make any noise.

As they cut their way through the thick growth, they toted along
binoculars for spotting the animals, altimeters for measuring their
height above sea level, thermometers to measure the temperature,
and compasses to let them know exactly where they were. When
they spotted gorillas, usually from high above the animals on the
hillsides, they noted the exact locations and circumstances as measured with all these instruments.

Sabater-Pi watching gorillas in the forest of Río Muni (Paul A. Zahl, National Geographic Society)

Jones and Sabater-Pi found that the rivers that cut through the forest, as well as the new roads, had trapped the gorilla groups into small home ranges because the animals feared crossing water. Then they compared the gorillas' ranges with those of the chimpanzees who share the forest. They found that the gorillas preferred the forest's edge, where thickets of secondary growth made attractive gorilla food, while the chimps lived in the center, eating fruits like figs that grow in the primary forest.

These scientists found that the lowland species passed its days very much like the mountain gorillas, with travel-feeding in the morning and afternoon, broken up by a long midday rest, and bedtime at dusk. They found that lowland gorillas, like their mountain cousins, lived in groups of between two and twenty members, and that their nests, as well as the sounds they made, are almost identical.

What differences they noted reflect the differences in their forests, the biome. The mountain gorillas that live where it is cold love the sun and seek it out. The lowland gorillas prefer shade, where they can escape the more intense heat. They even make their nests so that they face southeast, where it is cooler.

Sabater-Pi observed that the nests varied in design. Some were substantial and built in the trees. Others were very crude, barely nests at all. And he noted that often the gorillas built nests as though out of habit but then slept outside them on the ground. This led him to believe that gorilla nests are vestiges, a kind of leftover habit from a time when all gorillas were tree dwellers. Some gorillas just don't bother with nests at all anymore.

Few hagenia or vernonia trees grow in these forests, so the gorillas have adapted to a different diet. Many have cultivated a taste for fruits like bananas or sugar cane. But most of the time they eat aframomun. Three species of this shrub make up more than 80 percent of the gorilla's diet. They love its acid-sweet green fruit, as well as its buds and blossoms. They eat it all, fruit, shoots, and blossoms, then bend down its branches to build their nests.

Ecologists call the balance between gorillas and aframomun an excellent case of *mutualism*. For after the gorillas have slept in its branches and eaten from it, the aframomun seeds pass through their intestinal tracts, out their bodies as waste, and take root to grow into new thickets elsewhere in the forest.

Scientists have noticed only small behavioral differences between the gorilla species. These lowland animals don't soil their nests as regularly as the mountain gorillas, but this may be because of the different foods they eat. Another difference is harder to explain. The mountain gorillas go to sleep as the sun goes down. But the lowland animals often stay awake into the night, beating their chests. Scientists and trackers alike have heard the muted drumming, a strange music without vocal accompaniment, that fades away within two hours after sunset.

Sabater-Pi did not name the individual wild gorillas he followed, nor did he identify them by personality. That was not the aim of his study. But he did name each of the captured gorillas, ranging from two months to four years old, that passed through the Ikunde Center. He studied these individuals closely and charted careful records on each youngster's gradual acceptance of captivity.

So when Snowflake arrived in Bata, covered with red dust from the long walk to town, Sabater-Pi had a standard against which he could study how the albino adjusted in comparison with the black gorillas who had gone before him.

Like Joe a century earlier, Snowflake struggled desperately at first. Nonetheless, Señora Sabater-Pi forced him into a bathtub and then locked him in a cage about a yard high, wide, and deep. Freshly scrubbed, he looked especially appealing. But Snowflake did not seem to appreciate the attention he received.

Like Joe and all other captured gorillas, Snowflake snarled, scratched, and bit whoever approached his cage. He especially fought all attempts to touch his body. But unlike du Chaillu, neither Sabater-Pi nor his wife expected gratitude or affection from the small animal. At the same time, they did know that the young gorilla needed affection from them. So they gradually began scratching his head, then stroking his back until finally he let them hold his hand.

It took awhile for Snowflake to enjoy the advantages of civilization. First he had to endure its cures. His droppings held the eggs of intestinal parasites, a common problem among lowland gorillas; so he had to take antibiotics that left him clean, but weak.

Then an ophthalmologist looked at his blue pink eyes and found that they contained no pigment. Like most humans with light eyes, especially albinos, Snowflake blinked twenty times a minute in light that was shady. In bright sunlight, Snowflake blinks almost all the time. Because of the lack of pigment, his retinas receive excess light that dazzles him.

After the run of examinations, Snowflake stayed in his small cage all day except for an hour each in the morning and afternoon, when he was brought out to eat meals and to get to know his captors. Before he could leave the center, Snowflake would have to get used to different foods and to human beings.

But Sabater-Pi could afford to be patient. Snowflake had lapped down a pan of milk his first day there, so he knew Snowflake would not starve no matter how stubborn he might be. The milk alone provided all the protein he needed to survive.

Snowflake, however, was not very stubborn. After barely a week he let his keeper scratch his head. Another week passed, and Snowflake could be seen following his caretaker around. A few more days, and he took his keeper's hand and happily escorted him on his rounds.

The charts show that the normally colored gorillas crossed this imaginary line of happy adjustment after at least thirty days of captivity. But Snowflake managed it in half that time. After twenty-five days at the center, visitors could see Snowflake sitting outside his cage, clapping hands and turning somersaults, eager to tempt a human friend to play with him.

By this time Snowflake had given up his diet of aframomun fruit and ripe bananas, and was enjoying baked breads and biscuits. He was eating human foods after only two weeks in captivity. The normally colored gorillas had usually taken at least twice as long to change their eating habits.

Snowflake followed the pattern plotted for the other gorillas, but

Snowflake with a friend after he has learned to live with people at Río Muni's Ikunde Center (Jorge Sabater-Pi, National Geographic Society)

he adjusted more easily to the ways of humans. This may simply reflect a personality difference between Snowflake and the others. Or it may mean that Snowflake's poor vision had left him an outcast in his gorilla group, so that he was more receptive to human attention than a normal black gorilla would have been.

6

Snowflake and Arthur Riopelle

Scarcely a month after he arrived at the Ikunde Center in Río Muni, Snowflake was ready to fly to Spain. There he exchanged his boxlike cage for a room in the zoo veterinarian's home, and later a luxury suite in the primate house of the Barcelona Zoo.

But his life as a part of scientific record was only beginning. Dr. Riopelle now began to commute between his own laboratory in Louisiana and the Barcelona Zoo. He did not want to miss the unique chance of observing an albino gorilla grow up. He wanted to compare Snowflake's development with a normal gorilla's and find out if being white had any effect on Snowflake's growth or behavior.

Once again Snowflake had to endure physical examinations. While scientists regularly weighed him and measured his hands and feet, doctors checked his eyes, confirming his supersensitivity to light.

Because human albinos are often also hard-of-hearing, Riopelle devised a test to discover if Snowflake's ears were impaired. Since he couldn't take him into a soundproof testing room and hook him up to earphones, Riopelle settled on softly calling out Snowflake's name amidst the babble of zoo noises. Snowflake was always easily distracted from his play, and Riopelle deduced that his hearing was fine. Besides, Snowflake rumbled the same soft pig-grunts while eating as the wild gorillas made. And he would do that only if he could hear himself.

When Snowflake moved to the zoo, he found a companion waiting for him. Muni, a black male gorilla, was almost exactly his size and age, a perfect playmate. This was an ideal research situation, because the two animals were both wild-born, male, and a little more than two years old. The only visible difference between them was their coloring.

The two gorillas, one black, one white, shared everything. Together they slept in a little back room, where neither one objected to the nearby window that let in the harsh glare of a streetlight or the clanging and banging from the city docks.

They climbed up each night to the cement shelf that cantilevered out from the wall, and after a moment of sitting, they lay down, head to toe on the edge of the shelf, and fell asleep.

They never seemed to miss the nests they must have slept in as tiny babies. And only Muni remembered how to build one when the scientific researchers gave them branches. This may mean that Muni's memory was better or that his mother, but not Snowflake's, had built nests. Or it may mean that Snowflake is just one of those lowland gorillas for which nest building had passed to a vestigial or outgrown skill. But neither gorilla ever tried to sleep on the floor, a memory perhaps of nights above the ground in the sodden rain forests.

In the mornings, they would tumble down a chute leading from their bedroom to a large indoor cage, where ladders, wheels, and shelves gave them plenty of chances to play. And then, if they felt like going outside, they followed another chute out into a large round patio with high red-tiled walls.

Six months passed. Snowflake seemed happy in his new life, and Muni did too. But the young gorillas had already developed very different personalities. Snowflake seemed to crave human attention. He was exceptionally affectionate with his keepers, and he was especially vicious towards Muni, whom he bit and scratched, whenever the keepers tried to pay attention to him in Snowflake's presence.

From the start Snowflake loved the crowds. Like a seasoned actor, he waited for his audience to gather, then leaped and pranced to their applause. While Snowflake worked the crowd, Muni played gorilla games, chasing around the cage, swinging and exploring his zoo world, heedless of the people beyond the bars.

Snowflake had arrived a celebrity. His face peered from the cover of *National Geographic* magazine, and a Spanish toy manufacturer turned out small stuffed miniatures of the white gorilla. Perhaps Snowflake was just responding to his fame. But whatever started it, he became addicted to all the attention.

His relationship to people, however, was quite unlike his relationship with the small black gorilla who shared his life. When the research team examined the animals, they turned out to be equally intelligent and, with the exception of Snowflake's vision, equally robust. Yet they played very different roles.

Snowflake might attack Muni if the keeper gave him too much attention, but alone in their cage, Muni called the tune. When their four pounds of bananas, two pounds of apples or pears, half a pound of ham or chicken, and loaves of bread appeared in the cage every afternoon, Muni always got first pickings.

When they played horse, Snowflake always rode passively while Muni got to choose the way. Or when they danced together face to face, Muni set the pace. When they play-wrestled, as young gorillas do a great deal of the time, Muni clearly took charge, deciding where they would go, how complicated the holds should be, and just how long the game should go on. It seemed as if Snowflake deferred to Muni, no matter what.

Dominance occurs in many primate groups. Baboons and chimpanzees as well as gorillas follow a single leader. Among wild gorillas the silverback sets the tone for his group, leads them to good food supplies, and decides where they should rest and when they should play.

Snowflake and Muni playing in their cage at the Barcelona Zoo (Michael Kuh, National Georgraphic Society)

The other gorillas acknowledge their leader by letting him have the best food. And if they should happen to meet him on the ground or on the branch of a tree, the submissive animal gives the leader the right-of-way.

The research team had not started out to examine dominance as a part of their study of Snowflake and Muni. But it is a question that interests all students of primate behavior. Dominance played an important role in evolution, and it may play an important role in the future of the gorillas as well. A good leader controls his group, solves petty squabbles, and protects them from dangers.

In the wild, the dominant male may inherit his position as the eldest son of the most important female. Age is very important in primate hierarchies. But in the zoo, the scientists had a chance to explore dominance and submissiveness in a different setting.

Muni and Snowflake lived in a perfect democracy. Like immigrants to a new world, neither had "family" connections or an inherited position. The observers were curious. Was Muni simply naturally dominant over Snowflake? Would he always be, or would their relationship change as their needs changed?

Snowflake and Muni were three years old when Riopelle began thinking about dominance, and Muni was already clearly in charge. If Snowflake had some food in his hand and was just about to bite into it, all Muni had to do was reach out and Snowflake would stop in mid-bite and hand it over without a fight.

The scientists did most of their work by simply watching the daily lives of the gorillas. But once in a while they decided to test the youngsters in a controlled situation. One day, for example, they strung a wire across the top of the walled patio and dangled a golden banana which they could pull up and down.

When Muni saw it, he did not hesitate but jumped for the prize, over and over. Snowflake waited on the sidelines, his elbows on his knees. He waited patiently until Muni was ready to let him take a turn. Snowflake never jumped alongside Muni. He never competed. When he was alone, however, he tried as eagerly as Muni had to grab the food.

But dominance is more than winning in competition. In the wild the dominant animal braves new situations and is unafraid to venture down strange paths. So the scientists decided to introduce some surprises to the two young gorillas.

First the six-year-old son of one of the members of the research team who had been playing with the small gorillas frequently walked into the cage wearing a gorilla mask. Snowflake stared at him for five minutes before he understood the trick. But Muni whipped off the disguise right away.

Then the team decided to try something more exotic, and they chose a mirror. Very few animals besides humans are able to understand the concept of their reflections. Even among the apes, each individual animal reacts differently to the sight of its mirror reflection, photograph, or television image.

No one could guess how the gorillas would respond to the full-length rectangular mirror that suddenly appeared in their cage. Muni noticed it right away and moved towards it. At almost the same time, Snowflake backed away. Muni tapped the mirror gently at first, and then grew bolder. Soon he was playing, looking at himself with his head between his legs, then standing upside down with his legs balanced against the mirror. Finally, he sat down and took advantage of the mirror to inspect the soles of his feet and other parts of his body that he had never seen before.

And all the while Snowflake hung back, frightened yet fascinated at the same time. He was familiar with his reflection in the glass wall of his cage when the sun hit it just so at a certain time of day. Yet this was clearly different. He eyed the mirror from a distance and tried to busy himself in a different part of the cage. But the mirror drew him like a magnet to a certain point. It was days before Snowflake finally went up to the mirror, looked at his face, tapped it softly, then ran away.

It had begun to seem that the observers could predict all of Muni's and Snowflake's behavior. Fearless Muni approached strange objects; timid Snowflake cowered and ran. The next test seemed to confirm this. The scientists left a human doll in the

Muni examines his feet in the mirror. (Michael Kuh, National Geographic Society)

Snowflake discovers himself in the mirror. (Michael Kuh, National Geographic Society)

patio, leaning against the tile wall. Muni reached out to touch it with the back of his wrist. As it toppled over, Snowflake jumped back. But Muni leaned further over to watch it closely. Then Muni sniffed at the doll, pulled its arm, picked it up and ran, swinging it until he reached the center of the yard, where he proceeded to take it apart.

Snowflake followed behind, watching Muni all the time but never trying to touch the doll.

A few days later the scientists introduced another toy into the patio. But this time it was one of the small stuffed white gorillas that were on sale at the zoo shop. They propped it up against a rock and waited for action.

As usual, Muni reached it first, sniffed, touched it, and dragged it around the patio. Then the keeper took it away and held Muni back. It was Snowflake's turn to explore the new toy.

Snowflake walked over in his familiar slow way, sniffed it, and then picked it up and tossed it onto his shoulder like a sack of potatoes. Muni had been watching and approached Snowflake. Snowflake tucked the toy gorilla under his arm securely for the first time, and ran off.

Muni soon caught up with him, and after a short struggle managed to retrieve the prize. But things had changed. Muni had treated the toy gorilla exactly the same as he had treated the human doll. But to Snowflake, the toy white gorilla was more than something to look at, take apart, and toss away. Snowflake did not pull at it. Instead, he sniffed at its bottom as he would sniff at another gorilla's. And as Snowflake continued to play with the toy gorilla for the next few days, he began treating it like a female gorilla, as if he could have a sexual friendship with the miniature of himself.

Muni still tried to take the stuffed toy away from Snowflake, but Snowflake fought to keep it. And although Muni still usually won, Snowflake's behavior had changed.

The final test came when they locked Muni inside the cage and left Snowflake outside in the patio. The keeper then carried in Afenengui, a thirty-three-pound female, just half the weight of both five-year-old males. The keeper sat her on the first level of the jungle gym. Snowflake perked up immediately, approached her, then followed her about. She fled in fear, teeth bared in a snarl, but Snowflake continued to trail after her, reaching out to touch her in an affectionate way whenever he got the chance.

The next day it was Snowflake's turn to remain inside, and

Snowflake cuddles the toy gorilla. (Michael Kuh, National Geographic Society)

Muni was let out to meet little Afenengui. Muni made the same ardent advances, and she rejected him with the same snarls.

On the third day, both Snowflake and Muni greeted the small female on the patio. Each animal still wanted her for himself, yet without a fight, Muni retired from the competition. Snowflake claimed Afenengui. Their roles had reversed. Snowflake had become the dominant male.

The scientists watched as the leadership slipped from Muni to Snowflake. They had learned that at least between these two gorillas, dominance is not permanent. The magic ingredient seemed to be motivation. Snowflake had not bothered to exert himself over a banana or even a doll. But when it came to another gorilla, a female gorilla, the prize had prodded him into asserting his will.

Snowflake and Muni were still only half grown when they took part in these experiments. But they were growing rapidly, and soon they were too large to be weighed, measured, and manipulated.

Years passed, and Muni died.

Snowflake found a new cage mate, the female Ndengue, who has already had three of his babies. The infants are all black, but each one carries an albino gene. When these gorillas are old enough to have babies, and if they want to mate with each other, there is a 50 percent chance that one baby will be white. Then a new generation of albino gorillas may grow up again in Spain.

7   **Miss Congo**

The vast green amphitheater of the saddle area on Mount Kari-simbi soaked up the July sunshine one afternoon in 1925. Drops of rainwater clung to festoons of orchids and helped camouflage a gorilla group that was strung out along the slope, feeding on succulent stalks of wild celery.

A leopard's cry broke the stillness, followed by the scream of a young gorilla in distress. The lead silverback snapped alert. In seconds he had gathered his youngsters and females together, except for one straggler who kept on eating.

This small female gnawed at the thick stem, unaware of the huge party of human hunters who had been walking for seven days from the shores of Lake Tanganyika just to find gorillas. Their false cries had diverted the rest of the group, leaving her easy prey. The hunters closed in, grabbed her, and brought her to their camp. Soon they were moving down the steep mountainside, leaving the lush saddle forest she would never see again.

On the way to Stanleyville, capital of what was then the Belgian Congo, other unlucky gorillas joined the caravan. One was a handsome blackback, at that time the largest gorilla ever captured. He fought the men so furiously that they had to restrain him with ropes at night. Tragically, this cost him his life, for one morning his trappers found him dead, a victim of flesh-eating ants that had devoured him alive as he lay writhing in bondage.

At Stanleyville, the 175 African trackers dispersed to their homes. By the time the gorillas reached the seaport on the Atlantic coast, only the Americans, Ben Burbridge and his son, remained to accompany the young female, which they had named Congo, and the other surviving gorilla, a small male called Marzo, on the long voyage to Europe.

This was Burbridge's third African expedition. He had retired young and rich from selling Florida real estate. Now he devoted his time and enthusiasm to capturing African animals. He had managed to trap some gorillas on earlier expeditions, but this was the first time any of them had survived.

Ben Burbridge liked to boast that he was a friend of the animals because he hunted with cameras as well as guns. And he brought back the first motion pictures of the wild, along with a collection of skins and tusks. He was also proud that he had perfected the technique he used to nab Congo: diverting the gorilla troop, rather than the usual approach of shooting the mother to take the infant.

The first leg of Congo's westward journey took her to Marseilles. There Burbridge learned that the French had a law forbidding wild animals on passenger trains. But they did allow dogs to travel if the owner rented a whole compartment and crated his pet. Because he had to cross France to get to Belgium, where he had promised to leave Marzo at the Antwerp Zoo, Burbridge found a large wicker clothes basket and painted the French word for *dog* in large letters on the outside. Then he put the two small gorillas inside.

As they crossed France, different train conductors checked the crate, and each was eventually convinced that the small apes were an odd kind of dog.

In Antwerp, Burbridge arrived with his thirty-five trunks, his bundles of lion skins and elephant tusks, and his clothes basket of gorillas, at a small hotel. At this point he opened the basket to give the animals some fresh air, and like twin jacks-in-the-box, they leapt out and created chaos in the hotel lobby.

Eventually he got them back in the basket, and a few days later left Antwerp with just Congo. Now she traveled all alone in a small square cage on the F deck of the White Star liner *Homeric*, while the Burbridges stayed on the A deck as they sailed for New York. But the trip was choppy, and Congo grew so seasick that the purser took pity and moved her forward, away from the ship's engines.

She arrived in New York a celebrity. She was not only the first female gorilla ever captured, but the first mountain gorilla as well. However, she was too sick when the ship docked to face the crowd of reporters and photographers waiting at the pier.

Burbridge faced the press himself. He explained that he had spoken to Miss Congo, as he always called her, in the central African dialect he assured them she knew very well. Then he described his adventures and announced that Miss Congo was for sale: the price—$20,000.

Then Burbridge moved with the young gorilla into New York's Hotel Pennsylvania. Twenty-four hours later both Burbridges were hospitalized, suffering from tropical infections. And Miss Congo settled into the east wing of the Central Park Zoo's red-brick monkey house.

Word soon came by telegraph that Marzo had died in Antwerp. Miss Congo was now the only gorilla, male or female, lowland or mountain, in captivity anywhere. Yet no buyer spoke up. So Burbridge cheerfully accepted his brother's invitation to bring Congo to Shady Nook, his estate on the shores of the Saint Johns River near Jacksonville, Florida.

The southern American climate was damp like that of the African mountain rain forests, with torrential rains falling one out of every five days. It was more temperate than Africa, as the days ranged from 45 to 90 degrees Fahrenheit, and the nights seldom fell below freezing. Congo seemed to thrive there.

Yet she remained unsold. Burbridge was asking a lot. In 1925 baby chimpanzees were going for 500 dollars each. And although gorillas were more exotic, they were also notoriously less healthy. No one seemed ready to risk the cash. While he waited for a buyer, Burbridge's sister-in-law, Juanita Burbridge, coddled and indulged Congo and called her, in the slang of the 1920s, her Gorilla Flapper.

As a flapper, Miss Congo lived in gorilla luxury. The Burbridges built her a house-cage not far from their cottage. It was twenty feet long, ten feet wide, and eight feet high. About a third of the cage was roofed over and floored, to serve as Miss Congo's bedroom, into which they tossed fresh straw every night so she could make herself a nest.

They fed her three meals a day, offering the little gorilla cooked bananas, yams, and apples, to make up for the wild celery and berries they couldn't find in Florida. Miss Congo grew rapidly. Several months after her arrival, she had grown from 40 to 120 pounds. And three times during her first year there, she had to have a new metal collar fitted around her thickening neck. In spite of all the attention, Congo was a prisoner. She either lived inside a small cage or was locked into a collar and chain when she went outside every day to play on the manicured lawn or climb the limbs of the sturdy American live oaks near the river.

She had no hope of a gorilla companion. For solace she sought out the Burbridges' pets: an Airedale named Betty, and Bobby, a bulldog. She also seemed to enjoy human friends, especially a neighbor down the river who came over daily to roughhouse with her on the lawn.

The neighbor was wrestling with her one day when, in order to get some pictures, he unlocked her chain and they moved down towards the river, where there were no shadows. Miss Congo surprised everyone then by dashing out onto a long dock and tumbling six feet off the end into knee-deep water.

Young Congo had probably never known a deep river on Mount Karisimbi. Shocked by the dunking, she ran all the way back home to the security of her cage.

Whether they were feeding her or letting her play near the

water, the Burbridges made up the rules as they went along. No one else had ever kept a female mountain gorilla, so they had to guess what was best, at least until they got some expert advice.

By November 1925, Miss Congo had managed to set a record. She had been captured when she was about five, old for learning new ways, and four months later, she was still alive. She faded from the headlines after her move to Florida. But the popular press never forgot her and brought her back to the front pages when they discovered that she was to become the subject of experiments by the famous Yale psychologist Robert Mearns Yerkes.

Yerkes had gained national fame because of his pursuit of two new psychological problems—the questions of IQ tests and the mental ability of animals. Yerkes called his science *psychobiology* because he studied what he believed was the evolution of conscious behavior. Yerkes would be using Miss Congo to investigate both intelligence and animal behavior at the same time.

During World War I, as a member of the government's National Research Council, Yerkes had suggested a new way to process the thousands of young men who lined up at military bases all over the country. Yerkes developed tests similar to those of Dr. Alfred Binet in France. He confidently believed that the tests could measure each man's intelligence so he could be placed in a job suitable to his abilities. As a result of this mass testing, Americans got used to the idea of IQ tests.

As for apes, Yerkes had been fascinated with them for twenty years. There were no animal behavior laboratories in the 1920s. It was Yerkes himself who suggested that studying primates under controlled conditions might help us learn something about their behavior. He believed that studying those animals closest to humans might eventually reveal something about human behavior too.

Yerkes had confined his studies to small mammals until 1914. Then he accepted an invitation from an ex-student who had moved to southern California and set up a makeshift laboratory with some monkeys and a small orangutan. Yerkes took a train to the West Coast and there devised a series of tests to measure the orangutan's curiosity, his mechanical skills, and his ability to solve problems.

Yerkes was very excited by his results and anxious to compare them with tests on the other great apes. He wrote to Wolfgang Köhler, a psychologist who had a colony of seven chimpanzees on Tenerife (one of the Canary Islands, at that time a German possession), and Köhler sent him an article he had just finished writing about the chimp study.

Both psychologists approached their ape subjects the same way. They tested their skills with boxes, ropes, pulleys, and other mechanical contraptions.

In 1923, Yerkes had a chance to buy a pair of chimpanzees from the Bronx Zoo in New York. He took them to his summer home in New Hampshire. When they were not building nests in the New England woods or playing with Yerkes' daughter Roberta, he put the young chimps through the same series of tests. But soon the chimps died, and Yerkes was apeless again.

Then on Thanksgiving Day, 1925, a phone call interrupted him in his laboratory at Yale. It was a friend of Ben Burbridge's, asking him if he would like to work with Congo in Florida. Yerkes left home almost immediately, afraid to miss this unique opportunity.

Within a few days he met the young gorilla. He was careful. He didn't want to scare her, so he started off very slowly. He treated her like a small child, allowing her to explore his face and hands with her fingers, her nose and her mouth. Soon she reached out from behind the bars of her cage and put her arm around his neck. They were friends.

The Burbridges allowed Yerkes a lot of freedom with Congo. And they followed his advice and changed her diet, removing the chocolates and cookies that Juanita Burbridge loved giving her pet. The only limit the Burbridges set was that Yerkes had to stay on their estate and use their facilities.

Usually a psychologist gets his tests ready before the subject enters the room. That way it is all a surprise. But with Miss Congo, Yerkes had to set up his apparatus while she watched. Soon the setting up became part of the experiment. Congo seemed to enjoy watching the preparations, and when she could, she even helped.

Yerkes accepted these few limits. He knew he had to take advantage of Congo while he could, for she was still for sale. He wasted no time, and measured Congo's physical skills and made notes on her temperament as well as her intelligence.

After the first Florida winter, Yerkes published the results of his work. He returned to Shady Nook in the winters of 1927 and 1928. In the spring of 1928, Burbridge finally found a buyer, and Miss Congo went to join John Ringling at his circus's winter quarters in Sarasota, Florida.

Yerkes managed to follow Congo's development for two and a half years. He always reminded himself that Miss Congo was just one specimen of a highly intelligent animal. He knew that he should not generalize too much about all gorillas from her performance. He also took into account that her capture in the forest and her trek by land across Africa, and by sea to Europe and America where she lived in a cage isolated from all other gorillas, must have left emotional and perhaps intellectual scars that would affect both her temperament and her behavior. Keeping all these obstacles in mind, he put Congo through a long series of tests that resulted in a book Yerkes published in 1927 called *The Mind of a Gorilla*.

8   Miss Congo and Robert Yerkes

During Dr. Yerkes' visits, Congo ate her supper at dusk, then went to sleep until dawn. Yerkes would show up about eight-thirty, having eaten breakfast before he came. But Congo had to wait to eat. As Yerkes explained, the Burbridges provided their gorilla guest with free room only. They paid for her food too, of course, but they made her earn it. And that meant concentrating on the varied tasks that Yerkes gave her every day. These were usually prying open locked boxes, hauling food in on ropes, or in some other way figuring out how to obtain a reward.

Instead of a breakfast eaten all at once, Congo's morning meal consisted of tidbits of baked apples, bananas, and yams spread out over the five-and-a-half-hour testing session. But life in the wild had never included three meals a day, so this was no hardship for her.

All of the tests took place either inside her cage, where Yerkes had installed a removable grid through which she could poke her hands, or on the broad lawn next to the river. Wherever they were, Yerkes wrote down everything. There were no tape recorders then, and the new movie camera that Yerkes loved to use did not film indoors or under rainy skies.

What Yerkes lacked in technological tools, he made up for in experience, and in the data he had already collected from the orangutan in California and the chimpanzees in New Hampshire. Now he used the same careful procedures, noting everything he observed about Congo, whether or not he could explain it.

Perhaps that was part of his genius as a scientist. He weighed Congo and examined her fur and her eyes. When she refused to let him get a good look at her teeth, he wrote that down too, observing that all of his other apes had been perfectly willing to let him probe inside their mouths.

Altogether, after meeting Miss Congo briefly at the end of 1925, Yerkes spent about six weeks at a time with Congo in 1926, 1927, and 1928. And during these visits he presented her with a wide assortment of problems, all aimed at describing her intelligence, which Yerkes defined as the ability to adapt to new situations.

At first he felt disappointed. The five-year-old gorilla he met in 1925 seemed sullen, withdrawn, and dull. Yerkes was accustomed to chimpanzees and orangutans who used their long fingers to get into all sorts of things. Like many scientists of his time, Yerkes had assumed that manual dexterity was a sign of increased intelligence: that the hand was the cutting edge of the mind.

But when he gave Congo a problem such as a padlocked box with some food inside—the same test that he had given the other apes—she did not even try to use her fingers. Instead, she attacked the lock with her knuckles, pushing and shoving until by sheer force she broke it. Yerkes was so amazed at this clumsiness that the only word he could find to describe her approach was *fumbling*.

Yerkes knew that the way an animal used its hands was important. A lot less was known about the geography of the brain in the 1920s than we know today. Handedness, the tendency of a person or a primate to use one hand more than the other, seemed to be an attribute of many primates. But it had never been really studied in a gorilla.

Today, neurobiologists who are studying the structure and the function of different parts of the brain believe that handedness is directly connected with what they call the *laterality* of the brain.

All primate brains, including the human brain, are divided virtually in halves. In humans, these hemispheres are not the same. The left temporal lobe in the left hemisphere is usually slightly larger than the right one. The halves, moreover, have separate functions. In general, the left half of the brain controls the right hand, and the right half controls the left hand. In right-handed people our unique human power of speech is mainly controlled by the left hemisphere, while appreciation of space is the right hemisphere's job.

Moreover, there seems to be a connection between laterality and the ability to think abstractly. There is some evidence that gorillas share this trait with humans. Congo seemed to use one hand more than the other. And in a collection of gorilla skulls collected by Fossey in Rwanda, there is a marked difference in the size of the hemispheres, which may reflect the size of the brain it once protected. The difference in size may simply show that these particular gorillas chewed more on one side than on the other, and consequently developed larger muscles near the sagittal crest to work with larger jaw muscles. Or it may mean that gorillas have brains that are like our human brains and, at least in some instances, can be said to reason.

Yerkes himself just gathered the data. He did not apply the question of handedness to the problem of describing a gorilla's mentality. Most of Yerkes' work involved detailed descriptions of how Congo reacted to new situations.

All of the tests he devised used some bait or lure to entice her to work. When he had tried the same tests with the other great apes, Yerkes had found the chimpanzees and orangutan always predictable. But Congo fooled him.

Some days she worked quickly for her rewards. But other days she ignored what had seemed like a favorite food the day before. Sometimes she worked for one treat but not another: for an apple instead of a banana, or a whole fruit but not a half of it. Other times she concentrated deeply for no reward at all. She might even ignore the treat after she had won it, anxious, it seemed, to return to try the task again for its own sake.

The probability of failure sometimes seemed to discourage her from even trying. Conversely, when she was succeeding, the experience of the success itself seemed to spur her on.

One of the series of tests Congo tried was the same one Köhler had used on Tenerife. Congo sat inside her cage, and Yerkes put an apple on the ground outside. He placed it just far enough away so that she couldn't reach it when she stuck her hands through the grid. But when he left a stick inside the cage, Congo quickly picked it up and used it to reach the apple and shove it within her grasp.

Later he hid the stick so that Congo had to search for it in order to get her apple. She started rummaging around, looking for the tool, convincing Yerkes that she had "foresight," the ability to plan ahead.

Sometimes Congo contemplated a problem for a while, then solved it in a flash. Yerkes strung up a half-inch manila rope between two vertical iron posts outside her cage, and attached an apple to the farthest end of the rope. Congo started to reach instinctively towards the apple but stopped midway when she apparently realized it was too far away. Then she climbed up on her bench, beating her chest intermittently, and stared at Yerkes. Minutes later she suddenly seemed to get the answer. She climbed down, grasped the nearest part of the rope with her right hand, pulled it up, then hand over hand moved the rope until she had hauled in the apple.

Yerkes believed that these instances of problem solving, not through trial and error, but through an apparent flash of understanding, revealed a quality he called *insight*. Other psychologists had argued that insight is unique to humans. But Yerkes insisted that if you could call this sudden "catching on" in human children *insight*, then you would have to use the same term with apes.

Whether these flashes were insight or not, Congo seldom had them. More often, Yerkes just waited for her to solve a problem

Congo uses a stick to push food to where she can grab it. (From *The Great Apes,* by Robert M. and Ada W. Yerkes, Yale Univ. Press, 1929).

by herself. When she failed, he showed her how. At these times he found her incredibly slow. Then suddenly she would do something clever. Yerkes admitted that he found himself surprised at every turn during his study of Congo.

Another series of tests brought Congo out of her cage down to the live oak on the lawn where she played most afternoons. Yerkes attached a long chain to Congo's collar and then wound it twice around the broad, bulky tree trunk. Once again he placed the reward just far enough away so that Congo had to unwind the chain in order to get her food.

Congo surveyed the situation, then stood up, picked up the chain and carried it, like a lady going to market, around and around the tree trunk. She seemed to grasp this problem immediately. So Yerkes decided to try it again. This time he anchored her to a different oak tree several yards away across the grass.

The new situation stymied her. Congo spent an hour there, apparently confused, before she unwound the chain.

Yerkes was perplexed, but not as much as he was by the next tree problem. This time he suspended an orange from the highest limb, and he left some wooden crates scattered on the lawn.

Congo anchored to her favorite tree on the lawn of the Burbridge estate (From *The Great Apes,* by Robert M. and Ada W. Yerkes, Yale Univ. Press, 1929)

Congo was usually clumsy with her fingers, so she amazed him when she went straight to the crates, piled them into a pyramid beneath the food, climbed up, and took her reward. The chimps had been especially clever with boxes, but Yerkes had not expected Congo to catch on so quickly.

Fortunately Yerkes was able to return to Jacksonville a year later. At six years old, Congo was just entering adolescence and had doubled in size and strength. The wooden poles she had used as props in 1926 had to be replaced by metal ones. And her personality had altered too. Instead of hanging back, she actively

Congo piles wooden crates on top of each other so that she can climb up to reach a treat suspended from a tree. (From *The Great Apes,* by Robert M. and Ada W. Yerkes, Yale Univ. Press, 1929)

sought out human company. But the biggest surprise of all was Congo's reaction to him.

She stared Yerkes directly in the eye for two minutes, a rare gaze from an ape that avoids direct eye contact most of the time. Then she helped him remove the grid which had been in place inside her cage since he had left the year before, and she hunted up a stick which she pushed through the bars. She clearly remembered him and the games they had played together.

She still used her hands as if they were encased in baseball mits. But she used them deliberately now and with greater success. In 1927 Congo improved her performance on most of the tests she took again. But none so mysteriously as the chain around the tree trunk.

Yerkes led her again to the distant oak tree. Now she picked up the chain right away and solved in seconds what had taken more than an hour the year before. Yerkes wrote that it seemed to him as though she had spent the year mulling over the problem and now had the solution in mind.

After his third visit, Yerkes and his collaborator and wife, Ada, began completing the tremendous volume in which they included everything that had ever been known about the great apes. At the end they drew up comparisons among the three species. When they came to gorillas, they almost always referred to the experiments with Congo.

They realized that intelligence is too complicated to define as one thing. So they tried to separate it into its different qualities, qualities that, when added up, make an intelligent being.

One of the qualities they singled out was "curiosity." Yerkes observed that Congo never destroyed the things he had brought to her. Once he even suggested that if he had left his new hat in her cage overnight, he would be sure to find it in one piece come morning. Any chimp would have taken it apart. He recalled that when his daughter Roberta was small, she too had specialized in destroying the toys she explored. He proposed that there must be a connection among curiosity, destruction, and learning. One of the good signs that he observed on his trip in 1927 was that Congo had become more destructive, although she never took things apart as thoroughly as the other apes.

Another quality of intelligence he discussed was "imitation." He observed that chimpanzees, orangutans, and children all seem to learn by imitation. When a chimp sees a man hammering on a nail, all you have to do is give him his own hammer and nail, and you have an ape carpenter. But Congo never imitated her captors. Yerkes felt this was a weakness in her species that cut them off from adapting to a new environment and that might be forcing them into extinction. Later on, when he had a chance to examine more gorillas, he found that they did imitate and that Congo alone had just been slow in that particular skill.

Yet in some ways, even Congo surpassed the other great apes. She had a much longer concentration span, and Yerkes felt that the ability to concentrate was absolutely essential to good behavioral adaptation, one of his own definitions of intelligence.

Above all, however, Yerkes was impressed with Congo's memory. She clearly recognized him from year to year. Moreover, she remembered the things they had done together.

When he thought about Congo, Yerkes discovered that her one constant was her inconsistency. The weather, as well as the people with whom she had been playing and the moods of the two small dogs, seemed to affect her work. All these were intangibles that he knew had something to do with the way she behaved, but he could not easily enter them onto a graph.

Yerkes never understood Congo. He suspected that she was capable of a craft and cunning far beyond anything he had seen in the other apes. He also suspected that she was deliberately concealing her insights from him.

But oddly enough, when he summed up his comparisons of the great apes, Yerkes seemed to set aside the results of his own tests with Congo. He recorded honestly that chimpanzees and orangutans had performed more skillfully with their hands. He admitted that they were easier to teach than Congo, that they imitated humans more readily. Yet something about Congo left him uneasy.

Yerkes assumed that some mental processes went on inside her head. But when he commented on her thinking, Yerkes was quick to point out that he sensed things in Congo that he could not prove.

Perhaps, he suggested, mountain gorillas are slower than lowland gorillas. Or maybe Congo was duller than most members of her species. He did not add what he might well have included: that she might have been too old, beginning at five, to respond to his teaching. Recently scientists discovered that when gorillas, orangutans, and chimpanzees were tested together, the most "brilliant" performance was turned in by a two-year-old orangutan. The others seemed to slow down with age.

Whatever the reasons, Yerkes disregarded the evidence. He admitted that although he had no facts to back him up, he suspected that of the three anthropoid apes, the one with a mentality most closely approaching our own is the gorilla.

Yerkes never had the chance he hoped for to follow Congo through her maturity. She lived only a short time after the move to Sarasota to join the circus. In April 1928, she died of what her faithful newspaper following called a "broken heart."

At the time of Congo's death, Yerkes returned from Florida convinced that it was a better place to keep primates than cold, rainy New England. A year later, under the auspices of Yale University, he opened a primate laboratory in Orange Park, thirty miles south of Jacksonville, where he gradually collected monkeys, chimpanzees, orangutans, and finally, gorillas.

Always ready to travel to meet an ape, Yerkes went to San Diego, California, in 1949, to test three baby gorillas that the naturalists Osa and Martin Johnson had given to the zoo. These later studies seemed to confirm his suspicions that gorillas are at least as clever as their ape cousins.

When Yerkes died in 1956, the Florida laboratory had grown into the world's single largest collection of captive apes. Yale decided that they could no longer keep it, but fortunately just at this time, the federal government planned a series of primate research laboratories and made the one in Orange Park part of the project. They moved the staff onto the campus of Emory University in Atlanta, Georgia, in 1964, and renamed it the Yerkes Regional Primate Center, in honor of the scientist who began it all.

Other scientists are working at the Yerkes laboratories today and are continuing to study the great apes. In the 1960s, Dr. Duane Rumbaugh began a project at the San Diego Zoo, in which he matched groups of chimpanzees, orangutans, and gorillas in special intelligence tests. Rumbaugh took advantage of the advances made in psychology since Yerkes worked with Congo. And he also had many more animals than one lonely gorilla to work with.

Robert Yerkes attributed Congo's sudden ability to solve problems to insight, a sudden understanding with no apparent reason. It was as if the subject had suddenly said, "Aha! That's it!" But Rumbaugh expresses the apes' apparent capacity for complex learning in another way. He repeated with the great apes the ingenious experiments done in 1949 by Harry and Margaret Harlow, which showed that in both monkeys and children, learning comes step by step.

These tests depend on visual perception. The subjects are given the task of selecting the odd object, perhaps a plastic square from a choice of a square and several circles, in order to win a reward. Or they are challenged with selecting the correct object (the one with food hidden under it) from a pair of objects, over and over again, using hundreds of different pairs. At first the subjects all fumbled. But soon they learned where to look and seemed to be showing insight. The Harlows believe that these moments of "Aha's" that look like insight are really the result of a lot of accumulated experience. The Harlows called their tests *learning sets*. They discovered that both monkeys and children learn to learn, moving from simple sets to more complex solutions.

Rumbaugh refined these tests with his ape subjects at San Diego. After each group had learned a series of instructions, he reversed all the signals. Where they had been rewarded before, they now received nothing, and where before there had been nothing, now there were rewards.

His results would probably not have surprised Yerkes. Rumbaugh discovered that the three great apes performed better than all the smaller monkeys. He also discovered that although the three apes performed almost equally, the one species that outperformed the others was the gorilla.

Rumbaugh pointed out, without making any real judgment, that the apes seemed to perform in direct proportion to the weight of their brains. The chimp with a brain of 390 cubic centimeters to the third power (cc^3) came in third, the orangutan with a weight of 425 cc^3 came in second, and the gorilla weighing in at 525 cc^3, still a third the size of the average human brain, came in first, among apes.

All the evidence is still not in. Rumbaugh is quick to point out that there are more unknown than known facts about ape abilities. Like humans, gorillas are probably influenced by their mothers and their habitat, as well as their genetic traits.

Congo spent the first five years of her life in a world that none of us can ever know. Captured, she brought with her a demeanor and behavior that convinced one of the leading psychologists of his era that she was indeed a wise and cunning creature.

9　Assumbo and Mamfe

Assumbo's naked belly rubbed against his mother's warm, hairy body as he twisted his dark head, searching for her nipple. In the nineteen hours since his birth, Assumbo had tried to suckle at least twenty-two times. But his mother, Nandi, did not help him, and twice, when he had her nipple partly in his mouth, she had pushed him away.

Nandi lay exhausted on the concrete floor of her cage. Her labor had been much longer than usual for a gorilla because Assumbo had been twisted about. Nandi struggled the long night of July 14, 1973, and on into the next day, until Assumbo finally arrived. And while she labored, a closed-circuit TV camera allowed the public to watch from inside the mammal house at Britain's Jersey Zoo. At the same time, the zoo staff, including honorary director Gerald Durrell, watched privately from inside the old manor house where they had their offices.

They watched anxiously as Assumbo emerged. At first he was still. Then he squirmed—proof that he was alive. Now the observers waited for him to nurse. They hoped, above all, that Nandi could care for her own son. But Nandi was just too tired, or perhaps her nipples were so tender that it hurt her to let him suck. The staff watched, hoping. They were reluctant to take the tiny baby from her because Nandi seemed protective and might be a good mother. But Assumbo had to eat.

So when the little gorilla was twenty-eight hours old, they loaded a capchur pistol with an anesthetic dart and knocked Nandi out. The keeper waited until she was quite asleep, then opened her cage door and reached gingerly in. He prodded her legs to be sure she was unconscious. Satisfied that she was, he snatched the day-old infant. From then on, Assumbo's life would be shaped by the human beings who would hand-rear him nearby in the nursery, replacing his gorilla parents.

Everything was ready there, just in case. The small room held an incubator, a washbasin, and bright Disney cutouts on the walls. A local pediatrician who usually examined only human babies waited to examine Assumbo. Throughout his first week, all the people who came into the nursery sterilized their hands and arms, and wore surgical masks to protect the infant from infection.

The second day of his life, Assumbo met his foster father, young Jeremy Usher-Smith, who held him while he drank his first meal from a bottle. Assumbo weighed in at 4.5 pounds, a good size for a gorilla infant. He had spent 270 days growing inside his mother: about 10 days less than most human babies, and he weighed a few pounds less than the average newborn human.

When Nandi awoke, she did not seem especially disturbed that Assumbo was not there. She had been born in west Africa, but she had lived in captivity on Jersey, an island in the English Channel, since she was two. She had never seen a gorilla mother care for an infant, and she may not have known what to do with Assumbo.

It is hard to guess what would have happened to the infant in the wild. She might have let him die because she was so tired. Or she might have been preoccupied with feeding herself and let him nurse despite the pain, because she would have been used to seeing gorilla mothers feed their babies.

Meanwhile, Assumbo thrived in the zoo nursery. The temperature there was kept at 70 degrees Fahrenheit, a good deal warmer than the night air in Trinity Parish on the north end of the island. The Jersey climate is cooler than Nandi's birthplace in the Cameroons. But the channel island is a lot warmer than the zoo in Basel, Switzerland, where Assumbo's father, Jambo, was born.

Assumbo's lineage is distinguished. On his father's side, he is second-generation captive-born because his father, Jambo, born in 1961, was the first male gorilla born into captivity. Assumbo's birth was a triumph because the Jersey Wildlife Preservation Trust, where it occurred, is no ordinary zoo but a sanctuary dedicated to preserving and breeding endangered species.

The trust had Jambo on loan from Basel so he could mate with Nandi and also with N'Pongo, Jersey's other female gorilla. Twenty years earlier such a loan would have been unthinkable. As recently as 1956, no gorillas had ever been born outside the wild, and many zoologists believed they never would be. But at the end of that year, a female gorilla was born at the zoo in Columbus, Ohio. Three years passed before the second captive birth occurred. Then Jambo's sister arrived in Basel. Since then about 300 gorillas, all members of the lowland species *Gorilla gorilla gorilla,* have been born in captivity; more than half of them are still alive.

But this population boom is scant compared to the drastic decrease of wild gorillas, who continue to be the victims of hunters and farmers. So each zoo birth is crucial. And the zoo personnel hover over each infant. Many of the infants do not survive, so several months passed before the Jersey staff had the time or the energy to relax and celebrate.

Meanwhile, Assumbo grew. When he was a week old, he lay clutching a small terry-cloth towel for comfort inside his incubator. At five weeks, a small tuft of white hair sprouted on his rump, the sign of ape infancy, which is like a flag in the wild, telling all other gorillas to "be gentle" with the baby.

Soon Assumbo grew out of the incubator and moved into a basket. Then he moved into a wooden playpen filled with toys. That day could have been a terrible one for the small ape. He was bigger than anyone anticipated, and when he stuck his hand through the bars and reached out, he accidentally burned himself on a nearby radiator. His skin blistered and peeled, and the new skin grew back slowly. But Assumbo did not complain. He continued playing happily as it healed, apparently tougher, or with a higher threshold of pain, than a human baby.

When Assumbo was almost two months old, another event took place to which he did react. He had spent his first weeks basking alone in undiluted attention. But on this day he turned around to discover an incubator in the nursery. Inside it lay Mamfe—his new half brother.

Unlike Assumbo's birth, which had been so closely watched, Mamfe just appeared on the concrete floor of N'Pongo's cage on September 11. He must have been born at night. His mother had cleaned him, then climbed up to the heated ledge of her cage and abandoned him. This time nobody thought about waiting and seeing.

Nor did they have to knock N'Pongo out. The keeper just opened the door to her outside area, and N'Pongo walked past her newborn son without a glance. Then the keeper grabbed Mamfe and rushed him to the nursery.

Mamfe was younger than Assumbo had been when he was separated from his mother. Left on the cage floor, he had lost a lot of his body heat because he could not yet regulate his temperature. The incubator, which for Assumbo had been cautionary, was absolutely necessary for his half brother.

The next day, Mamfe squealed a soft anxiety cry inside his incubator, and Assumbo joined in. From that moment on, many of Assumbo's actions were affected by his brother, and since then the two gorillas have seldom been apart.

Yet from the start, they were slightly different. Assumbo has always been shyer of people until they are familiar to him. His temperament has more extremes: quiet at times, then suddenly excitable. As he grew older, he would put on a display complete with stamping and chest beating after he had mastered a new skill. Assumbo gets on well with those people he knows well, and he is more likely than Mamfe to look them in the face and play quietly.

Assumbo and Mamfe as babies (Phillip F. Coffey)

Mamfe has always been constantly high-strung. He loves an audience, and he will hang from the top of his cage and do silly stunts to win attention from the crowd outside. He is also somewhat jealous of his older brother. When he was less than a year old and his foster father came to play with them in their cage every day, Mamfe devised a foolproof way of keeping all the attention.

He would climb up onto the six-foot-high ledge inside his cage. And then he would fall backward, deliberately, so that his human friend would have to leave Assumbo's side and rush to catch him. Each time he did this, Mamfe would giggle, get up, and topple over again.

Weeks turned into months, and in May, the staff moved both "boys" permanently from the nursery into a large cage where there was plenty of space for ropes and room to swing. All the while, their foster father kept careful records. He measured and observed everything they did, from the time each little gorilla first sucked his fingers, listened to a rattle, crawled, and stood up. He even noted Assumbo's first temper tantrum.

All the while, the pediatrician kept his own measurements. He compared Assumbo's and Mamfe's growth with that of a human baby boy. Starting at the top, he measured the circumference of Mamfe's skull right after he was born, and he discovered that the bones had already hardened. This is different from a human infant's skull, which does not grow solid for almost a year in order to let the human brain expand. Gorilla infants are born smaller than humans, but by the time they are eleven weeks old, they have usually doubled their weight. Human infants do not double their birth size for six months.

The doctor noticed that sometime between his third and fourth months, Assumbo's skull actually decreased around the middle. He thought perhaps he had made an error until the same thing happened to Mamfe's skull at about the same age. The doctor suggests that this may be when a male gorilla's skull grows taller, preparing the crown for the sagittal crest it will grow one day.

The doctor tested the gorillas' reflexes to compare them with responses he knew occurred in human babies. One of the reflexes found in newborn humans who think they are about to fall is to cross their arms in front of them for protection. This is called the *Moro reflex,* and it disappears after a few weeks. The gorilla infants feared falling even more dramatically. At any sudden motion, each one reached out to grasp anything with a much stronger grip and with both hands *and* feet. And the gorilla does not lose this reflex as humans do. Instead, it merges gradually into the gorilla skill of brachiating: hanging and swinging suspended from the branches of trees.

Assumbo's world centered on Mamfe, his human foster father, and the rest of Jersey's staff. But when he was ten weeks old, a new personality who was to become important to him in a different way entered his life. Psychologist Margaret Redshaw began visiting Assumbo once a month, and her visits meant a special kind of play to the small gorilla, for she was giving him a variety of toys to play with which were really tools for a series of psychological tests. These tests measured the way the infant gorilla learned to understand and act in the world around him.

Redshaw enjoyed her monthly trips to Jersey during the next three years. She had been born in the north of England, in Dur-

ham, and had grown up in the south, near London. With degrees
in psychology from the University of Manchester and University
College, London, she had already studied human babies to see
how they developed in early infancy.

Now she was prepared to *compare* the development of these two
kinds of primate infants, humans and gorillas. When she began
visiting Assumbo and Mamfe, she liked gorillas well enough but
did not especially know them. As her study moved through its
first, then second, and finally its third year, Redshaw developed an
enormous respect for Assumbo and Mamfe. As she got to know
them well, what had begun as one kind of study grew into something larger.

Margaret Redshaw with an infant gorilla named Bamenda at Jersey (Phillip F. Coffey)

But Redshaw never lost sight of her original goal. She was there to discover how tiny infants, both gorillas and humans, develop intellectual skills, by noting the way the infant acts in its own environment while its nervous system is maturing.

There are people who think it is outrageous to claim that animals can think at all. They create a wall between human beings and animals, and insist that only humans have conscious thoughts. But it is hard to ignore Redshaw's results.

She chose to use the tests and measuring scales that the Swiss psychologist Jean Piaget developed almost thirty years ago. At that time, as a young father, Piaget watched his own three children, Laurent, Lucienne, and finally Jacqueline, as they lay in their cribs, began to move about, and grew to become part of the outer world.

Piaget observed that all of his children (and, by implication, all human children) progressed through the same stages as their understanding grew. Piaget believes that normal human infants pass through these stages at about the same time. He also insists that all normal children move through these stages in the same order.

What is remarkable about the way Piaget describes learning is that he sees the maturing infant joining in and helping himself to grow. Just as a baby kicks and kicks to make his leg muscles strong, so the infant moves his eyes, his head, and then his hands to exercise his mind. The baby that is holding his fingers up and making shadows against the wall is learning to understand that he can control his own fingers, and he can control the shadows he is making with them.

Redshaw accepts that Piaget's stages describe all of childhood. But she feels that only the earliest stage, the one an infant goes through *before* it has learned to talk, makes any sense when you compare a baby gorilla with a human baby. This first period, starting at birth, lasts for a year and a half. Piaget calls it the *sensorimotor* stage because during these eighteen months, the infant is learning to use his senses—sight, sound, touch, smell, and taste. He is learning to coordinate these senses with his muscles as they grow stronger, so that he can sit, crawl, walk, and hold things in his hands (and, in the case of the baby gorillas, in his feet as well).

Redshaw wanted to find out if baby gorillas develop the same skills as humans and, if they do, if they move through the same stages as they become increasingly responsive. She wanted to discover if the small apes moved through these same stages in the same order and at the same rate of speed as humans do. She was looking for ways of thinking and developing that are typical of all Hominoidea, including us. She was also searching for ways of thinking that are exclusive to human beings.

If she could find a common pattern, she suggested at the start, this would argue that *all* thought processes evolve the same way. It would lend weight to the argument that there is a continuous line of mental development throughout primate life. And this leads to the rather startling idea that just as physical life evolves, so does consciousness.

10 Assumbo, Mamfe, and Margaret Redshaw

When Margaret Redshaw first arrived on Jersey wearing her bibbed dungarees and sweater—the uniform of those who work with gorillas—she carried with her a videotape machine, notebooks, and plenty of small wooden and rubber toys. She left the island's picture-book airport and went right to the zoo. She paused at the entrance to look at the statue of a dodo—an extinct bird—the Jersey Zoo's symbol, then hurried in. On her way she passed the gorilla cages—the places she would eventually know, from the outside and some from the inside, too.

But on this first visit she skipped the adult apes and went straight to the nursery to see ten-week-old Assumbo and two-week-old Mamfe. She was anxious to begin and eager to meet her tiny subjects.

She knew exactly what she was doing. Her first aim was to measure the babies' cognitive growth (the way they developed mentally) using Piaget's tests and scales, and their manipulative skills (the development of the ways they used their hands). In all

94

of the studies, she would compare the little apes with two new humans.

Although Piaget had already tested his own children, Redshaw needed to do the tests over again to be sure that when she compared her human subjects to the gorillas, she would be comparing exactly the same tests, administered by exactly the same tester (herself), using exactly the same toys. The human children are called *controls*, for they set the standard against which the little gorillas were judged.

Between her visits to Jersey, Redshaw was visiting Oliver and Sam, two little boys who live in London. The boys were about the same age as the gorillas. Both children are firstborn, and both live in ground-floor apartments. She tested them in their homes, with their mothers there, at that time of day when the boys were usually happiest and most eager to play. She used the same tests with them as she had with the gorillas, and then charted their performances and compared them on charts with the baby apes.

The tests started out simply. While Mamfe lay on his back, she moved a multicolored bead ring in an arc over his head. She wanted to see if his eyes followed it smoothly, slowly coordinating the eye movement with the tester's movement. A simple test, but what it measures is not at all simple.

Redshaw had divided up the skills she was looking for into four categories, or scales, which had been made up by the two American psychologists I. C. Uzgiris and J. M. Hunt. Each simple test, such as the one she had used to test Mamfe's ability to follow a moving toy, led to a more complex test on the same scale.

Mamfe was able to follow the beads through a 180-degree arc, a semicircle, when he was six weeks old. At the same age, in the next test, he would continue to gaze at the spot on the arc where the toy had disappeared from his range of vision. It would seem that he had already developed enough so that out of sight was no longer out of mind. But Mamfe still expected the toy to reappear where he had last seen it. This showed that he seemed to realize that the toy existed apart from himself. But at six weeks of age, he still believed that the toy had to exist in the place where he had last seen it.

Eight weeks after that, he was able to find a half-hidden toy. Another four weeks, and he was able to find a completely hidden toy, showing that he was able to remember something he could no longer see and also to give that something a separate place in time and space. This first scale showed how infants, both human and gorilla, learned to understand that objects beyond themselves are permanent, and that they exist separately in both space and time. During the first year on this scale, the gorillas were always ahead of the humans.

These stages occur very early in our lives, and all of us, apes and humans, have to pass through them as we grow. We take it for granted that this has happened, and we examine them only if something is wrong.

The second scale Redshaw used explored how the growing infants learned to tell the difference between what they wanted and what they had to do to get it: how to separate means from ends. She began testing how the baby learned to match what he saw that he wanted, with what he could do with his hands—hand-eye coordination. The gorilla infants started out ahead of the little boys here too. But after a few months, Oliver and Sam understood more about using an object such as a rake (a means) to achieve a goal such as pulling toys closer to themselves (an end) than the gorillas ever did.

The third scale measured the infants' growing understanding of how things, like toys, exist in three-dimensional space. The babies liked to watch things fall. They dropped food from their high chairs and peered down to see where it went. In a way, an infant begins quite early to learn the laws of nature, especially the law of gravity. In this scale, sooner than on the other scales, the gorillas moved along ahead of the humans and then lost their lead altogether.

Redshaw's last series of tests showed the babies' first understanding of cause and effect. At first both sets of babies acted as if they had caused all the events they were aware of. But later they changed. Oliver and Sam could get their windup toys moving again way ahead of the gorillas, either by winding them themselves or handing them to a grown-up to do it for them.

The charts show exactly what Redshaw learned. In almost every case, in the first few months the human infant and the gorilla infant did, indeed, learn things in the same order. But at the start, the gorilla babies learned everything sooner.

Redshaw began the more advanced tasks with Assumbo at the same time she was testing Mamfe's eye movements. But soon she would watch both gorillas learn to sit up and crawl. Gorillas do not learn sitting ahead of crawling, as most children do. The sequence is more varied. When gorillas do sit, it is always in a knuckle posture. One of the first times Redshaw saw Assumbo, he was trying to sit like that, leaning on the backs of his hands. She put a toy in front of him, and the small gorilla got so excited he moved his hands—and fell flat on his nose. Knuckle-balancing, sitting and later walking, is very instinctive in gorillas.

But when he reached his thirty-fifth week, Assumbo did what no human infant ever does. With both of his small hands cupped slightly, he gave part of a chest beat. He announced to the world that despite the cheerful nursery, the glass bottles, and the plastic toys, he, Assumbo, was a gorilla.

In other ways, too, the humans and the gorillas were always very different. Assumbo never really did learn to play constructively, to build with blocks. And perhaps even more telling about the way that human thinking differs from a gorilla's is the way that the gorillas always worked alone. When Oliver or Sam grew frustrated at being unable to help himself, he fussed and asked for help. Assumbo and Mamfe would watch a music box run out, and shake it to get it started. But they never handed it back to Redshaw for her to wind for them. Asking for help seems to be a strictly human talent.

Redshaw believes that the gorilla's inability to play constructively with objects and their lack of social behavior with each other or with their human companions are the two *key* differences between the apes and us.

The first year was eventful for both gorillas. After ten months they moved into cages, where the public could watch them all day long. And they enjoyed the company. Their human foster father continued to come in and play with them once a day, tossing and tumbling as a silverback would do in the wild, but at the same time disciplining them so that they would not grow too rough.

Before the year ended, Redshaw had suffered with Assumbo as he lived through the agony of breaking a tooth, probably while he was chewing on a plastic chain and swinging from the bars at the same time. As the exposed nerve in the tooth grew more painful, bewildered Assumbo began biting down on everything to ease the pain, including the psychologist.

Finally, a local dentist agreed that the tooth would have to come out. But he could not just make an appointment for Assumbo to come in and sit in his dental chair. Like his mother, Assumbo had to be sedated. Then, asleep, he had surgery. The dentist discovered then that baby gorilla teeth differ from human baby teeth. Even the baby teeth are strong. And the root of Assumbo's tooth reached down one whole inch inside his jaw.

Early in 1975, Redshaw continued testing Assumbo and Mamfe, but she had to make some changes. The small animals had become so fond of the psychologist that they liked playing with her too much, searching the pocket of her dungarees for the nuts she kept especially for them. She had to devise something to separate herself from them so that they would not be distracted and could concentrate on the tests.

The result was a screen, a plastic screen that fitted perfectly into the cage doorway. Small openings inside the screen allowed Assumbo and Mamfe to reach through and pick things up outside—if they wanted to. But they could not see beyond the screen, so they were not tempted by Redshaw's presence.

Hidden from them, she would set up tasks that they could work at, or not, according to their whim. If they preferred to go on wrestling or chasing each other, as they had been doing before she arrived, then they did that. She wanted their voluntary help.

And she usually got it. For these scientific tests were fun for the little animals. Sometimes she might put some grapes, nuts, or dried fruit inside a box. Then she closed the box with a simple lid which Assumbo and Mamfe took off in no time at all. Next she put more food in the box and added a series of latches, each more

Assumbo unlocking a box (Phillip F. Coffey)

complicated than the one before. But the little gorillas solved these tougher problems too, concentrating hard and working persistently.

These treats were extras. The zoo never let its babies fast beforehand, as Congo had done years before in Florida. But they did have to earn them by delving into the boxes placed in front of Redshaw's video camera. And here even after a year, the little gorillas did not always play fair. Mamfe still wanted what Assumbo had, and he did not hesitate to beg for or steal his older brother's rewards.

As she came to the end of the second year, the testing grew more difficult. Oliver and Sam in London, and the gorillas on Jersey, were moving swiftly in different directions. They had started out with the gorillas moving faster through the same learning stages, in pretty much the same order. But as they approached their second birthdays, the human children learned how to talk and walk upright, and how to play with symbols, using toys in make-believe situations. At the same time, the gorillas became more apelike, walking along on their knuckles, beating their chests, climbing and swinging from the tops of their cages, and building nests.

Another year passed. Both Nandi and N'Pongo produced new infants, a brother and a sister, which Redshaw included in her tests along with a gorilla born at Howletts Zoo near Canterbury, across the Channel on the south coast of England.

As she included more animals in her tests, her results grew clearer, and more valid scientifically because each new infant she tested confirmed the pattern. Nandi had still another baby with Jambo. N'Pongo did too. The full brothers and sister turned out to be almost identical in character and performance to Assumbo and Mamfe. But even the unrelated gorilla at Canterbury performed the same feats at about the same age.

Two-year-old Sam (opposite, top) *builds a block tower. Two-year-old Oliver opens a locked box.* (Psychology Dept., University College, London, and Margaret Redshaw)

Assumbo and Mamfe and their brothers and sister showed that gorillas grow more uniformly than human children. All of the gorillas learned to crawl towards a toy at about seventeen weeks. They all started to gaze lingeringly on a toy at about seven weeks. But human infants show much more variety than gorillas; some children begin walking at ten months, and others not until they are a year and a half.

After three years, Redshaw could answer all the questions she had started out with in 1973. Yes, gorillas do go through the same cognitive steps as humans during their first year. Yes, gorillas do go through them in almost the same order as humans, although the gorillas move faster at the start. And she pinpointed eighteen months as the critical age, after which the gorillas develop those skills that are valuable to forest-living apes, while the humans learn what they need to live in a verbal, cooperative civilization.

But Redshaw's interest in Assumbo and Mamfe included more,

Zaire (left) *and Tatu are included in Margaret Redshaw's tests.* (Phillip F. Coffey)

The development of visual pursuit and object permanence. Chart by Margaret Redshaw. (From *Journal of Human Evolution,* July 1978, p. 135)

| | SUBJECT'S* AGE IN WEEKS | | | | | | | | |
| | GORILLA | | | | | | HUMAN | | |
STEP	A	M	Z	T	Mean		O	S	Mean
1. Follows a slowly moving object through 180° arc smoothly	6	6	6	6	**6**		10	10	**10**
2. Gaze lingers at the point of disappearance of a slowly moving object	10	6	6	6	**7**		10	14	**12**
3. Finds an object which is partially hidden	14	14	16	14	**14.5**		26	22	**24**
4. Gaze returns to starting point on disappearance of a slowly moving object	14	14	16	14	**14.5**		22	26	**24**
5. Finds an object which is completely covered by one screen	18	18	24	18	**19.5**		34	34	**34**
6. Finds an object which is hidden under one of two screens	22	22	32	22	**24.5**		38	34	**36**
7. Finds an object hidden under one of three screens	30	30	32	26	**29.5**		38	34	**36**
8. Finds an object hidden under a number of superimposed screens	30	34	32	30	**31.5**		38	42	**40**
9. Finds an object following a visible displacement under one of the three screens	34	38	32	34	**34.5**		42	42	**42**
10. Finds an object following an invisible displacement under a single screen	38	38	36	38	**37.5**		42	42	**42**
11. Finds an object following an invisible displacement under one of two screens	38	38	36	38	**37.5**		42	42	**42**
12. Finds an object following one invisible displacement with two screens alternated	38	38	36	38	**37.5**		46	46	**46**
13. Finds an object following one invisible displacement under one of three screens	42	42	40	42	**41.5**		50	46	**48**
14. Finds an object following a series of invisible displacements under three screens	42	46	44	42	**43.5**		54	54	**54**

*A = Assumbo   Z = Zaire   O = Oliver
 M = Mamfe   T = Tatu   S = Sam

now, than these cognitive and manipulative tests. She had become fascinated by the ways the babies played, and she went on to use the same equipment—the videotapes and the toys—to explain the ways that the young animals learned to play together.

She watched the bouncy run gorillas use when they are playing, and the different expressions they achieve with their mouths: lips relaxed to make play-faces, or teeth covered in a threatening expression.

Gorillas do not cry or utter the many sounds that human infants make as they grow into the habit of speech. But Redshaw noted that from about seven months old, Assumbo would bite his five-month-old brother, and then both infants would sound a shriek. At about the same time, they would begin making a coughlike grunt, just as they do in the wild.

Redshaw watched their games as they grew. She taped their play, then observed the tapes many times in slow motion. Redshaw could see them beat their chests and slap the floor, and she realized that they were not just slapping chaotically.

There was a pattern. The little gorillas used slaps as signals to coordinate their games, their runs and lunges. If Assumbo set up a box between them, both animals raced around it. Both paused if the box fell down, so that one of them could set it up again. And then they beat the ground to signal that the game was beginning again.

Although gorillas play together like human children, chasing and tumbling, they do not share—cannot, apparently, give and take—toys with each other as human children do.

At three years old, the small gorillas left babyhood and became juveniles. They stopped beating their chests just any old time and began to save this special gorilla gesture for those occasions when they were especially nervous, uncertain, or very excited.

By now Jersey had had seven small gorillas and was expecting more. But another zoo in the middle of England, operated by the East Midland Zoological Society at Twycross, had just two—two females. They suggested that the two males, Assumbo and Mamfe, move there. Jersey agreed. Their human foster father got

Tatu plays with a music box. (Phillip F. Coffey)

them ready and accompanied them across the Channel to the Midlands. He left them there, a little sadly, and returned to his younger charges.

But Redshaw still visits Assumbo and Mamfe, bringing with her all of her testing apparatus. And they remember her and seem pleased when she appears. Mamfe, at three, was the first small gorilla to learn to stack his blocks into a tower. Now Assumbo stacks them too, and Redshaw is delighted.

Most of their play, however, is physical. Assumbo and Mamfe

toss about large plastic bread trays, sit in them, and put them over their heads. They sometimes make up complicated, newer games, and they include their two new friends, Eva and Biddy, in their play.

Twycross is colder than Jersey, but the gorilla house is warm and cozy. When it is too miserable outside to play, the animals can watch a color television set mounted high on a wall, opposite some special gorilla perches. Now these sophisticated animals delight in watching human games on television.

Gorillas grow up sooner than humans. Some begin to have

Four-year-old Mamfe standing at attention (Margaret Redshaw)

babies as young as nine, though they are usually a year or so older. Although Assumbo and Mamfe are still small, they will be grown up long before Oliver and Sam, who patiently, and sometimes not so patiently, took the same tests. At four and a half, Assumbo was a juvenile who weighed nearly 100 pounds. He still had to pass through subadulthood (six to nine years of age) before he would be an adult silverback weighing around 350 pounds. At that time, Assumbo and Mamfe may become fathers. Their children will be third-generation captive-born gorillas about whom we now know a great deal, thanks to their cooperation and the patience and imagination of Dr. Redshaw.

II   **Dolly**

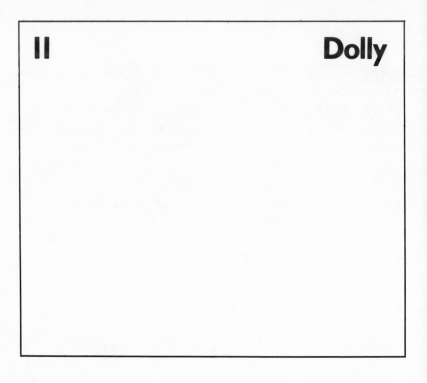

An infant gorilla who lost her mother somewhere in the forests of Zaire, in 1964, found herself in Brazzaville. Before she was ten months old, she had left that home too, to fly across the world to California. Still an infant, Dolly arrived at the San Diego Zoo, where she joined three gorilla playmates and a baby orangutan in the nursery.

There, as soon as she was big enough to play outside, Dolly began entertaining the children who came to watch her antics. She ran about in the play yard, with only a shallow moat separating her from her audience. Dolly always seemed to be ready for fun and full of pranks. Chortling beneath her breath, she usually gave herself away as she sneaked up behind one of her companions to push him or her into the water. Then, while her victim sputtered, Dolly would chuckle aloud as she ran for cover, stopping to peek back over her shoulder to make sure the people were still watching. She

Dolly enjoys a snack. (Ron Garrison, San Diego Zoo)

never went as far as the larger male gorilla, Trib, who almost drowned Roberta, the orangutan, by holding her head under water to stop her shrieking. Gorillas don't seem to like loud noises.

Although mischievous, Dolly was gentle, and she was chosen to be one of the first seven gorillas in San Diego to move to the zoo's Wild Animal Park when it opened in 1972 in the green San Pasqual Valley, thirty-two miles from the city. A new kind of zoo, the park maintains herds of animals that need open space, and breeds both endangered and more common species in its large, more natural enclosures.

Trib, now a young silverback, was among the group that shared the new green turfed enclosure for gorillas. He seemed to love its wooden play and shade structure and its shallow splashing pool. But above all, he seemed to love living with Dolly.

Six months after he joined her there, Dolly was pregnant. Then,

Trib, a gorilla (right), *with Roberta, an orangutan, in the nursery at the San Diego Zoo* (San Diego Zoo)

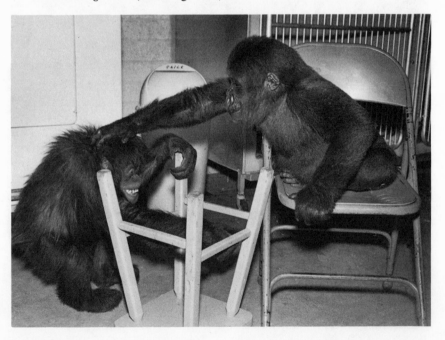

in October 1973, Jim arrived weighing six pounds and four ounces, the largest gorilla ever born in captivity.

Jim clung instinctively to Dolly, as Dolly must have clung to her own mother ten years earlier in the forest. But each time Jim's tiny hands grabbed her, Dolly pushed him away. Jim was strong, but he was no match for Dolly's approximately 180 pounds.

Jim was six hours old and getting tired. In spite of his healthy size, he still needed Dolly's warmth to maintain his temperature, and he was showing signs of growing cold. Yet she continued to resist him. Unfortunately the park staff had to remove him to the warmth of an incubator. Soon Jim was living in the animal care center of the Wild Animal Park.

The staff felt disappointed, but not surprised. Although chimps had been having babies in zoos since 1915 and orangutans since 1928, for half a century zookeepers accepted as fact that gorillas could not breed in cages. What few gorillas lived to maturity never reproduced. When females in captivity began having babies after 1956, they did not seem to be good mothers, and gorilla infants were almost routinely raised in zoo nurseries, like Assumbo and Mamfe on Jersey.

Vila, Dolly's cage mate at the Wild Animal Park, had already had one baby of her own in 1965, but she had not known what to do with her and could not be a model for Dolly. Today about a fifth of the nearly 600 gorillas in collections all over the world are captive-born. And 80 percent of them have had to be hand-reared. Often these were the lucky ones. Other captive-born gorilla babies have died from neglect and even from abuse.

Gorillas, like humans, have to learn social behavior, including how to mother. The babies instinctively grasp with their hands and feet. As they grow, they instinctively beat their chests. But gorillas do not know how to get along with each other unless they can follow an example. When a hand-reared gorilla does become pregnant, she is often at a loss about what to do once her baby is born and she has licked it clean.

Dolly had left her own mother before she had much experience being mothered. Perhaps equally important, Dolly had never had a chance to watch another gorilla caring for her baby. Wild gorillas often play "auntie" and "baby-sit" for smaller apes. Papoose learned from watching Petula with little Augustus, as well as from being among the other mothers who surrounded Uncle Bert at rest time, letting their infants tumble together in the sunlight.

Hand-rearing gorillas in zoo nurseries can be great fun for the zoo staff and for visitors who love to see baby animals close up. Little Jim got lots of attention. But hand-rearing perpetuates itself. And nursery-raised gorillas can become increasingly abnormal individuals as they lose contact with normal gorilla behavior.

The Zoological Society of San Diego hoped to have gorillas living in natural groups in the park: males, females, and their infants. If one mother gorilla could learn to take care of her own baby, she could bring it up socially healthy and at the same time provide a good example to the other females around her.

The zoo authorities thought about it, but there was no problem right away. Jim stayed in the nursery, and Dolly returned to her group. If Dolly had nursed Jim, she would not have become pregnant again for about three years. But now she was reintroduced to Trib, and within three months Dolly was expecting again.

This time the staff hoped Dolly would care for the baby, along with Jim, whom they planned to return to the enclosure as soon as possible. Somehow Dolly had to learn to mother.

The ideal way would have been for her to live with another gorilla mother that she could imitate. Then Dolly would have gotten used to the sights and sounds, the touch and even the taste of a baby. But there was no gorilla mother nursing her own infant in San Diego in 1974.

The staff tried a second approach. They cleared out the solarium, a large room in back of the gorilla compound where the gorillas sun when they are not on exhibition in the enclosure. Then they pointed a film projector against the rear wall. Many apes recognize themselves in pictures. They hoped that Dolly would learn from watching a feature film starring some photogenic gorilla mothers caring for their babies.

But Dolly ignored the colored scenes that flickered on the wall.

She found the sound and light from the projector much more interesting. It seemed that while practical experience was impossible for Dolly, learning from watching had failed, too.

They were left with one possibility—psychological training called *operant conditioning,* a systematic use of rewards to encourage specific responses to stimuli. Already five months pregnant, Dolly would spend the next three and a half months taking lessons in how to be a mother.

Steven Joines, a graduate student of anthropology and zoology at San Diego State University, volunteered as tutor. An animal lover, Joines had nursed sick raccoons in his Upland, California, backyard as a child, and he had spent two years in Scotland filming the elusive creature in Loch Ness.

Now Dolly's keeper, Ricky Cuzzone, introduced her to Joines as a friend. Then Joines spent the next few weeks personally winning Dolly's confidence with a combination of frequent visits, gentle speech, and red licorice strips. After a while Joines' footsteps on the concrete floor outside of her cage were enough to make Dolly rise and move to the bars to greet him.

Dolly was used to visitors. Cuzzone had been bringing her seven-month-old son, Jim, to exercise in the enclosure every day. Holding Jim up close, but still separated from her by the iron bars of her cage, Cuzzone would let Dolly reach through with her hands and nose to touch and smell him. As she carressed Jim, Cuzzone and then Joines would remind Dolly that Jim was a "baby."

So when Joines gave Dolly a burlap pillow and told her that it, too, was a "baby," Dolly recognized the word. She took the sack and held it gently. When Joines saw that Dolly did not bite or rip it, he made her a better surrogate baby. This time he shaped an armless, legless doll from cream-colored denim and gave it a definite head, which he marked in black with eyes, nose, and mouth. Although it did not look much like a little gorilla, Dolly seemed to like it and held it gently.

This worked so well that Joines soon tried giving Dolly a toy stuffed gorilla. She looked at it, screeched, and dashed away to

Dolly's denim baby (San Diego Zoo)

hide in an adjoining cage. The next day Joines returned the first, makeshift doll, and Dolly seemed happy again.

Seven days a week, four hours a day, Joines spent the summer of 1974 with Dolly. After a while he noticed her interest was flagging, so Joines shortened the sessions to twenty-minute intervals with long rest periods in between. Each morning he gave Dolly her doll, and each evening he took it away.

Now he began concentrating on her conditioning. One at a time, he taught Dolly to obey four different commands.

"Turn the baby around, Dolly," Joines urged her when she held the doll upside down with its face away from her body. Gorillas do not always instinctively hold their infants against themselves in what behavioral psychologists call the *ventral-ventral position*. Because gorilla infants are born with bare stomachs, they need to get heat from close contact with their mothers. Dolly had to learn that her infant needed her warm stomach next to its own, with its face turned toward her nipples, where it could suck.

"Pick up the baby, Dolly," Joines taught her next. And each time she did, he told her that she was good and gave her some soybeans or a slice of apple. But if she did not respond, he only repeated the command until she did.

"Be nice to the baby, Dolly," he taught her then. And Dolly held the denim doll carefully and rocked it.

"Show me the baby, Dolly," he asked her finally. And after about four days, Dolly had learned this command, as she had learned the others, and held out the doll for him to see.

Dolly learned each command separately, then practiced all four of them together every day. She never made a mistake then, and a year later, when Joines gave her the same commands, Dolly responded properly to each one.

By early September, Dolly had become an excellent mother, at least to the denim doll. Now the park staff prepared for Dolly to give birth. Joines did not want to miss the event, not after so much work, so he brought his sleeping bag to the park and began spending nights outside on top of her concrete cage.

But babies, including gorilla babies, have a special sense of timing. After weeks of nights under the stars, Joines had gone home for one good rest when, on October 2, 1974, approximately 250 days after the baby had been conceived, Dolly went into labor. Her keeper telephoned Joines to hurry back. But by the time he walked into the holding area, Dolly was sitting at the back of her cage, holding the baby.

Dolly recognized his familiar footsteps on the concrete floor and rose to walk upright to the bars. There, before Joines had caught enough breath to say anything at all, Dolly held out the tiny female she had just cleaned, and showed her to him.

Dolly began to care for her new baby, Binti, as warmly as she had rejected Jim the year before. No one had to remind her to "be nice to the baby." It is unclear how much the conditioning changed her attitude. Dolly might have been a better mother anyway this second time around.

Yet a few hours later, Joines got a chance to prove that his work had done some good. The denim doll had been quiet as Dolly

Dolly with her second baby, Binti, at the Wild Animal Park (San Diego Zoo)

practiced with it. But now Binti began to squeal, and the noise disturbed her mother. Dolly floundered as the infant cried until she heard the familiar command "Be nice to the baby, Dolly." And Dolly held Binti close, and the baby quieted down. She was off to a good start in the world. And so, they hoped, was the whole gorilla group in the park.

12   Ellie, Paki, and Patty Cake

Several hundred miles north of San Diego along the California coast, the Los Angeles Zoo acquired five small gorillas from west Africa all at once in 1965. They grew up together, two males and three females, in what seemed like an ideal situation for captive apes. All the animals appeared normal, and one of the females, Ellie, was especially good-natured and obviously attractive to the males who favored her. When Ellie became pregnant in 1972, the zoo hoped that Ellie would nurse her baby. But when the staff found the baby on March 19, 1973, its body had been mutilated. They assumed that the infant had been stillborn. Animal mothers often abort their first pregnancies or have dead babies, so the staff did not suspect anything seriously wrong.

Then on January 15, 1975, Ellie's second baby was found dead in her cage, its head separated from its body. Now the staff grew upset. The veterinarian could tell that this baby had been born alive, then decapitated.

But no one had witnessed the event. Ellie soon became pregnant a third time, and this time the staff watched her closely. But Ellie moved too swiftly for them. It was late in April 1976 that the humans stood by helplessly as Ellie bore her third baby and tore it apart before their eyes.

By this time they realized that Ellie was mentally ill. Perhaps her first baby had been stillborn and she had developed a distaste for it. There were certainly no clues in her earlier life to explain her behavior. Whatever it was, the curator believed it was too late to try to cure her deadly habit. So when in the spring of 1977 Ellie was pregnant for a fourth time, he decided to remove this baby before she had a chance to kill it. And the best time for that was before the baby was born.

The decision had been made, but the staff did not know when to operate. If they took the infant too soon, it would not be able to live outside its mother's body. If they waited too long, it would be born naturally and doomed to almost instant death. They decided to perform a series of amniocentesises, a technique used with human mothers in which doctors take a sample of the amniotic fluid that surrounds the infant in the mother's uterus. This fluid contains the infant's chromosomes, which doctors can analyze to discover the sex and health of the about-to-be-born baby.

When Ellie was tested on May 17, the fluid showed that the baby needed about two more weeks on the "inside." So on June 1, they knocked Ellie unconscious and brought her to the zoo's infirmary to take a final sample of her amniotic fluid. They waited all day until six that evening, when the laboratory reported that the baby's life systems seemed fine. Then the team of anesthesiologists, obstetricians, veterinarians, and pediatricians performed the first caesarian section ever on a gorilla. They removed the baby still in his birth sac and called him Caesar.

After two weeks, Ellie returned to the zoo's adult gorilla group, unaware that she had had a baby. She is an excellent breeder, however, and has already had another infant, Brutus, who was delivered the same way. She is helping perpetuate her species. But she will never have another chance to rear an infant.

And Caesar and Brutus will spend their first three years like human children. At birth Caesar went through the same routine

Ellie, Caesar's mother, at the Los Angeles Zoo (Sy Oskeroff, Los Angeles Zoo)

tests as a human baby in a modern hospital, and then he was placed in an incubator at the children's zoo. When he is three years old, the staff will try to introduce him to a group in the gorilla exhibition. From there he will be able to see Ellie across the concrete barrier. But he will never be able to touch her or know her as a mother.

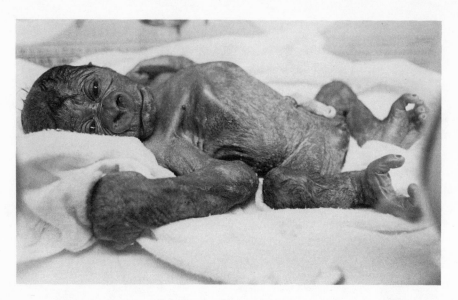

Caesar, twenty minutes old, in his incubator at the Los Angeles Zoo (Sy Oskeroff, Los Angeles Zoo)

Ellie's abusiveness is extreme and hard to understand. But other captive females have killed or harmed their infants by dragging them along concrete floors or actually tossing them about. These females do not seem to understand that they must protect and nurture their infants.

At the same time that Dolly and Ellie were adjusting to life in California, another lowland gorilla arrived on the East Coast of the United States. But Paki did not go to a zoo. As part of a group of nine gorillas, she went, instead, to the Yerkes laboratory which was then still in Orange Park, Florida. A few months later Paki moved with the other fifteen gorillas in the Yerkes collection to the campus of Emory University in Atlanta.

Life in a primate center is different from life in a zoo. Cages are smaller there, and not especially attractive. There is no crowd to please, and the scientists assume that the animals do not care about landscape design.

When Paki first arrived, all of the gorillas lived in pairs in the large animal wing of the laboratory. Until 1975, most of the Yerkes gorillas helped scientists who are interested in studying the physiological, medical, and chemical aspects of animal behavior. Here in these small cages, where they could control all the conditions, technicians took blood and urine samples from the gorillas and tried to trace changes in the samples to particular causes.

Starting in 1971, when she was eight years old, Paki became part of a series of experiments in gorilla sexuality. When she became pregnant in 1972, Paki spent most of her time with a female

Caesar at three months in the zoo nursery (Sy Oskeroff, Los Angeles Zoo)

cage mate until she was ready to give birth. Then she moved into a special cage where videotape and sound equipment were ready to record the event.

Paki's pregnancy provided Dr. Ronald D. Nadler, a physiological psychologist, with a chance to explore the connection between Paki's behavior and the chemical changes that occurred during her pregnancy. Then he was able to monitor exactly what happened as the baby was born.

Although many chimpanzee and orangutan babies had been born at the Yerkes Center, Paki's daughter, Kishina, was their firstborn gorilla. Nadler reports that Paki seemed to know exactly what to do when Kishina arrived. She cleaned herself first and then licked Kishina all over. But after that Paki seemed confused. It took twenty-four hours of awkward fumbling for her to get Kishina into the right position for the baby to suck. Yet when Kishina made soft sounds, Paki knew how to respond to them.

Paki might have become a good mother in spite of never having seen another gorilla mother, or any other adult gorilla, since she arrived from Africa when she was a year old. But two days after the birth, Paki had to be operated on to remove some birth membranes that had not come out by themselves.

When she returned to her cage after having been anesthesized, she began tossing Kishina across the floor as if she were a toy. Nadler could not risk waiting to see if the bond that had begun to grow between the mother and infant would return. He had to remove Kishina to save her life.

Curious about the peculiar problem that captive gorillas seemed to have mothering their infants, Nadler gathered information about all the ninety-four gorilla births that had occurred in captivity until then. He compared the information he got with what he knew about Paki. His results were complicated and not always consistent. But a pattern does emerge. When gorillas have babies for the first time, like Dolly and Paki, they do not usually care for them very well. But often these same animals are good mothers with their second or third infants.

Paki became pregnant again, and in April 1974, Fanya arrived.

Again Paki cleaned the baby, but this time she placed her in the proper ventral-ventral position immediately. Within a day, Fanya was nursing. Paki seemed to be as successful with this second baby as Dolly was with Binti in San Diego.

Nadler suggests that gorillas do have to learn from experience. But the kind of experience they benefit from is something more complex than watching another gorilla be a good mother, and something different from Dolly's conditioning. He suggests that during labor and then during the postnatal licking, the gorilla mother is establishing contact with her infant. The licking, especially, may create a bond between the mother and her firstborn. Then, even if she does not take care of this infant, she will remember the experience and form an immediate bond with all the rest of her babies.

This theory suggests that wild gorillas, too, may sometimes neglect their firstborn infants. It may mean that gorillas rely on the second and subsequent births to keep the species going. Or it may mean that in the unnatural world of the zoo or laboratory, female gorillas simply do not understand what is happening to them.

In March 1975, the Yerkes Center opened a new gorilla compound at its field station in the Georgia countryside. Here, in a grassy 100-by-100-foot enclosure, they moved in three adult male animals and then five females. They hoped to form a gorilla group which they could then observe to compare its social behavior with the behavioral studies, such as Harcourt's and Stewart's, taking place in the wild.

But a special series of events at the station in March 1976 added a new dimension to Nadler's study of mothering. In that one month, three of the females gave birth to their first babies.

One of the mothers had shared a cage with Paki and Fanya. She had perhaps learned from being with them, because she turned out to be the best of the three mothers. The other two females had been sharing a cage with each other. But the remarkable thing about the three new mothers is that all of them managed successfully with their firstborn babies.

Nadler suggests that isolating Paki in a concrete cage to protect her from infection and possibly from the other gorillas had been exactly the wrong thing to do. With companionship, these other first mothers have cared for their babies just as wild gorillas take care of their infants in the midst of a supportive family.

Gorilla groups in the wild range from as few as two members to twenty. In captivity as well, emotionally healthy gorillas do not have to live in large groups. When a pair of two-year-old animals, one male and one female, arrived in New York's Central Park Zoo in 1966, their only company was each other.

Caged together in the same red-brick house where Congo had stayed forty years earlier, Lulu and Kongo lived together until June 15, 1973. Then Lulu surprised everyone, including her keepers and visitors at the zoo, by suddenly producing a baby, Patty Cake.

The zoo separated Lulu from Kongo then, fearing that he would be rough on his small daughter. But Lulu began to ignore Patty Cake and seemed troubled. Yet as soon as the keeper allowed Kongo back into her cage, Lulu calmed down and paid attention to Patty Cake again. Gorillas seem to be better mothers if there is another adult gorilla with them.

Patty Cake lived with both of her parents during the day, but at night Kongo slept in a separate cage. One evening when Patty Cake was nine months old, she seemed to miss her father and reached out her arm towards him, through the bars that separated her cage from his. Somehow then, accidentally, Lulu yanked her, and Patty Cake's arm broke.

The keeper had to take Patty Cake away to have her arm set at the infirmary at New York City's largest zoo, in the Bronx. This was the first chance anyone had had to examine Patty Cake, and it was discovered that she had various intestinal parasites and a vitamin deficiency, and was generally underweight and undernourished compared to the nine-month-old nursery-reared gorillas.

Her arm mended quickly, and the zoo officials faced a decision. Should Patty Cake stay in the nursery in the Bronx, where her fur glistened with health and the added pounds gave her a rounded look, and grow up with other small gorillas? Or should they try to return her to Lulu and Kongo in Central Park?

The zoo needed advice and called on Dr. Nadler, who came from Atlanta to see Patty Cake. He weighed the young animal's chance for a normal life being hand-reared with gorilla age-mates against returning to her parents. Nadler advised them to continue giving her vitamins, since they now knew she needed nourishment, but to do this in Central Park, where she could grow up with Lulu.

When Patty Cake returned to the ape house, she stayed alone in her old cage for a while to get used to it. Then Lulu joined her. Though agitated at first, within twenty minutes she was holding her baby, Patty Cake, again. Soon Kongo joined them, and they are reunited now, a small, but normal gorilla family.

Across the country in San Diego's San Pasqual Valley, Jim has also joined the group at the Wild Animal Park. Dolly still cares for

Lowland gorillas at the Wild Animal Park—Aunt Vila with Jim at left, *Dolly with Binti* at center, *and Trib* at right (Ron Garrison, San Diego Zoo)

Binti, while Vila, the other female who joined the group when she was pregnant, to learn about mothering from Dolly, has adopted Jim as her own. He, too, is developing healthy social relations.

Each gorilla mother and infant is different, and each zoo and laboratory has tried in its own way to keep a healthy gorilla colony. But knowledge of gorilla behavior, both in the wild and in captivity, has grown dramatically since the first captive birth in 1956. Now captive gorillas all over the world are having babies regularly, and many have begun to mother their infants. Breeding is, of course, crucial for the continuity of the endangered species. And because so much gorilla behavior is startingly similar to our own, what we learn about maternal instinct, bonding, and mothering in gorillas may help us gain insight into these same areas of human behavior.

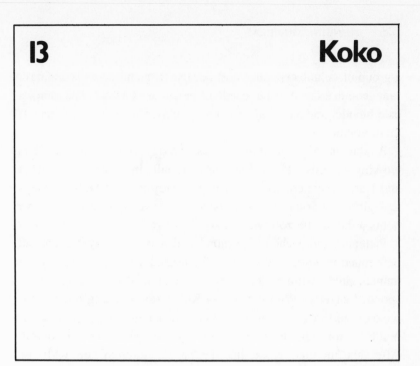

13 Koko

Fireworks lit the sky above San Francisco, and rockets boomed. It was July 4, 1971, and most Californians were celebrating the national holiday. But in the city's zoo up on Skyline Boulevard overlooking the Pacific Ocean, the staff celebrated another birthday. At four o'clock that morning, after five hours' labor, Jackie gorilla had had her baby. They named it Hanabi-Ko, which is Japanese for "firework's child."

Fourteen months earlier, another of the zoo's adult female gorillas had had a son. Jackie's daughter was the first female gorilla to be born in the zoo's gorilla grotto. Koko, as her name shrank to almost immediately, lived with her mother until December.

Gorillas are highly susceptible to intestinal diseases. In the fall, the little male had come down with dysentery-plus and had had to leave the grotto for treatment. Now Koko showed the same listless symptoms and also had to be taken, before Christmas, to the University of California's Medical Center in San Francisco. She never lived with her mother again.

When she returned to the zoo, she stayed in the nursery, where a group of volunteers could give her the frequent feedings and day-time companionship she needed. Francine (Penny) Patterson, a pale blonde graduate student from Stanford University, was one of these volunteers.

A student of developmental psychology, Patterson was then working towards a Ph.D. She was especially interested in language and learning experiments, and had already worked with monkeys and gibbons. Soon she was spending between eight and twelve hours a day at the zoo with Koko.

Patterson approached nine-month-old Koko the way Yerkes had befriended five-year-old Congo. She treated the small gorilla like a human child, winning her confidence gradually. And Koko responded eagerly. Within a month Koko was imitating one of Patterson's gestures, poking her thumb at her mouth to request her bottle of formula. Patterson knew exactly what she was doing. After six months, Koko had begun to communicate with her human friend.

As far back as we can see into history, people have yearned to talk with animals. The Garden of Eden boasted talking beasts, including the sly serpent. And folklore, legend, and fairy tales all include animals that speak. Yet it is only in the past 100 years that scientists have tried seriously to decipher animal sounds, especially those of the apes.

At the end of the last century, an American primatologist and linguist, Richard L. Garner, made a study of the ape "language." First he listened to the chimpanzees in New York's Central Park Zoo. Then he sailed for Africa to eavesdrop on the apes in their natural forests. He arrived in the Congo with a large number of green metal mesh squares, and as soon as he found a pleasant clearing in the forest away from all settlements, he laced them together. Then he filled this "cage" with canned foods, a camp bed, and a portable stove; climbed inside; and named his new home Fort Gorilla.

There he sat for months, listening and watching. For a short while he had the company of an orphaned small gorilla he called

STARTING FOR A STROLL

Richard Garner leaving his observation cage

Othello. Together they listened to the other gorillas rumbling around in the foliage.

Garner believed that the gorillas had a working language and that all he had to do to master its vocabulary was to listen closely. He jotted down every sound he heard in this mysterious tongue, but finally admitted that he could not translate the sounds or even spell them out in English letters.

Still, he felt certain that each sound Othello uttered had real meaning. When Othello died after a few weeks at the "fort," Garner returned to New York to analyze his findings in greater comfort. In all his time in the forest, he had isolated only four separate sounds, and only two of these well enough to repeat. The first, a whining followed by a deep sigh, Garner believed was an emotional signal that, he confessed, melted his heart whenever Othello used it. The second was the rumbling Othello and the other gorillas made as they ate.

Since then, scientists at Fossey's Karisoke Research Center have gone into the forests with battery-operated tape recorders. Many gorilla sounds are very low, almost beneath the range of the human ear. But the machine picks them up. Later, using an instrument called a Kaye-Sonogram, they transform the sounds into spectrograms: pictures on paper that look like the wiggly lines of a lie detector. Using this method, scientists have isolated between twelve and eighteen different sounds.

But these are all throat or belly noises. Gorillas do not use vocal cords or a voice box, nor can they shape sounds with their short tongues. They send immediate messages with these sounds, letting each other know that they are contented, or warning that danger is near. They do not seem to rumble, or pig-grunt, about what they plan to do the next day or to reminisce about the past.

This kind of communication, using a handful of sounds to signal immediate needs, is not language. Garner had assumed that the gorillas had a complete spoken language and that he could discover the key. But he was wrong. Although gorillas do communicate many things orally, they do not speak.

Since Garner's day, other scientists have tried to establish two-way communication with apes the other way around. As they could not decode the animals' sounds, they tried to teach apes to speak a human language, usually English.

Frustrating efforts began, usually with chimpanzees, which have always been plentiful in captivity. Chimps found their way into a surprising number of human households. And patient foster parents placed their hands on the chimpanzees' throats, shaped the chimps' lips with their own hands, and pronounced simple phrases repeatedly into the chimps' ears. After years of effort, one small chimp managed to say a few syllables. But it seemed clear that no ape could ever learn human speech.

Finally, in 1972, a scientist at the University of Connecticut discovered the physical explanation for this failure. Comparing the width of the throat (the pharynx) and the placement of the tongue of human babies with those of all three mature great apes, he discovered that in all four cases, the pharynxes were too narrow and too rigid to produce sharp sounds.

Human babies change enormously during the first eighteen months. By the time a child is a year and a half old, his pharynx has become flexible enough to shape the sounds that rise from the larynx into words. But the ape's nasal passages never change.

Language, spoken language, is beyond the physical capacity of nonhuman primates. And just as this point became clear, another group of primatologists remarked that many apes use a system of gestures among themselves. When a silverback nods his head, the whole group follows his lead. As linguists pondered the mystery of how language began among early humans, some suggested that perhaps a language of gestures—hand signals and head nods— might have been the way early humans communicated before we had spoken language.

They pointed out that even today, when spoken language is so important, we still use some "body language." Certain gestures seem to be understood by everyone: gestures such as holding out an upturned hand to beg or putting a finger across the lips to mean "quiet." Apes do not have human vocal cords. But they do have expressive hands with thumbs and fingers very like our own.

A large portion of the cerebral cortex of the human brain controls the movement of our lips and tongues and our hands. Children with hearing who are born to deaf parents learn to gesture before they learn to speak. If the hand is the cutting edge of the mind, language can be as possible in gestures as it is in sounds.

Among humans, there is a group that uses a system of gestures as a language. They are the deaf. One of the languages deaf people in the United States use is the American Sign Language, or Ameslan. An Ameslan "speaker" uses hand gestures called *signs* instead of words. Many of these signs are iconics, visual representations, like charades, of what words mean. Hands held together cradling stands for *baby,* and touching the mouth with a thumb extended from a fisted hand means *drink*.

Other signs, such as for someone's name, have no special symbolic meaning. Anyone who learns Ameslan has to learn fifty-five signal units and the individual signs for special things. Soon a person strings these signs together into sentences.

Two American psychologists, Allen and Beatrice Gardner, arrived at the idea that the great apes, which cannot communicate with their voices, might be able to learn a gesture language. The Gardners chose Ameslan instead of making up a gesture language of their own, because it is a real language. And if an ape could learn to speak Ameslan with its hands, then the psychologists could compare the way the ape used the language with the way deaf people do.

They began their experiment in 1966 at the Washoe County campus of the University of Nevada. They used a year-old, wild-born, female chimpanzee, whom they named Washoe.

The Gardners raised Washoe in a house trailer apart from all other chimpanzees. And reasoning that human children learn to talk because they hear speech all the time, they exposed the small chimpanzee to sign language as much as possible. They deliberately avoided speaking aloud in front of her, so that Washoe had to concentrate with her eyes alone to watch their hand messages.

They encouraged Washoe the way a human mother encourages

her baby. The praised each word and repeated each sign, gently correcting her if she made a mistake. By the time Washoe was five, she had a vocabulary of 132 signs, and knew enough grammar and syntax to keep up a steady "conversation" with her human tutors.

Since the Gardners' success with Washoe, psychologists have taught Ameslan to a whole generation of infant chimpanzees. At the same time, other scientists have taught different forms of language to other chimpanzees. Duane Rumbaugh, at the Yerkes Regional Primate Center in Atlanta, developed a computer system with a typewriter console that lets his chimpanzee Lana press buttons with symbols on them to create sentences in a new language he calls *Yerkish*.

Chimpanzees dominated the world of "talking" apes for a long time. This was partly just convenience. Chimpanzees are cheaper than other apes, and there are more of them. Chimpanzees also have a reputation for liking and imitating people. And chimpanzees are smaller than orangutans and gorillas, and seem less threatening.

Even among people who ought to know better, gorillas have a bad reputation, and many psychologists have avoided working with them. They do grow large. An adult male can reach 500 pounds in captivity, and many people are frankly scared of them.

Others, however, had dismissed the gorilla as a possible student because of Yerkes' tests with Congo. They ignored the recent tests that show gorillas to be at least as clever as the other apes. They pointed to Yerkes' results and reasoned that since gorillas are both poor at imitating people and poor at using their hands to manipulate things, they would be poor students of a hand language.

But gorillas have always had their champions too. Those who work with them find gorilla infants especially affectionate. And those who take care of them always mention the gorillas' subtle sense of humor. Gorilla advocates have longed to prove that the gorilla's mental abilities are at least equal to those of the smaller, high-strung chimpanzee.

But finding gorillas to work with is hard. An endangered species, they are now unavailable from the wild. And zoos guard their specimens, anxious to get them to reproduce.

Experiments like Redshaw's with Assumbo and Mamfe on Jersey measured the gorilla on its own terms. Assumbo and Mamfe would have played with toys whether or not Redshaw was testing them. Redshaw did not teach them new skills, nongorilla skills. She explored their abilities to find out exactly *what* they did naturally and *when* they did it, as they matured.

Patterson's project with Koko is altogether different. She is trying to unlock a gorilla's potential to see what Koko can learn under special conditions. She is hoping to find out what, in particular, Koko could never be able to learn if she were not being carefully reared in a special enriched environment.

Patterson knew the project was risky. Koko could suffer from being separated from other gorillas. There is some evidence that gorillas who grow up alone develop abnormal behavior, especially antisocial habits which prevent them from ever getting along sexually when they are grown. But Patterson believes that this unfortunate pattern may be the fruit of the zoo's failure to let animals get used to each other slowly.

There was also the risk to herself. Raising an animal that will grow up to have at least twice the strength of any human can be dangerous. The gorilla might not be able to learn to control her strength. She could unintentionally harm the people with whom she worked. But Patterson was ready to take these risks and needed a gorilla to teach.

Koko happened to be in the right place at the right time. She had been separated from her mother for medical reasons and needed vast amounts of human attention to be nursed back to health. When she responded so quickly to Patterson's Ameslan gestures, the zoo director, who was then Ronald Reuther, allowed Patterson to continue her project.

Reuther convinced the Zoological Society to buy Patterson a house trailer very much like the one the Gardners had used and moved it to the San Francisco Zoo. Soon Patterson had recruited her own volunteers, many of them deaf, who worked with Koko days, and most nights as well, in the trailer. Koko learned rapidly. In October 1974, Reuther gave Patterson permission to take Koko away from the zoo to be closer to the university. Now it was up to her adviser, Stanford University Professor of Psychology and Psychiatry Karl H. Pribram, to find the money to buy the trailer from the zoo and have it moved to its present location in Palo Alto, where the experiment could continue.

14

Koko
and Penny Patterson

Penny Patterson was used to living on a university campus. Born in 1947 to a professor of psychology at the University of Illinois, she grew up in a large family. Helping care for her younger brothers and sisters, she later realized, had helped prepare her to raise one healthy young gorilla. At Stanford, Patterson moved into the pale blue five-room house trailer set up on blocks in back of the campus art museum, near the anatomy building.

She had become interested in apes and languages after hearing the Gardners, who were visiting Stanford, describe Washoe. Patterson wanted to repeat their experiment using a gorilla, and at the beginning she followed the Gardners' examples.

The Gardners had tried different ways of teaching Washoe hand signs before they settled on the way that worked best. They call it *molding,* and it is a way of actually taking the ape's hand and bending the fingers into the right form, molding them.

Patterson did the same with Koko. She shaped Koko's hand until Koko got the sign right, although at first she had to ward off

Koko's attempts to bite her. Gradually the young gorilla stopped resisting, and soon she could learn a "molded" sign in just a few minutes. But unlike the Gardners, Patterson also spoke to Koko in English at the same time. Koko's experiment is different, then, from Washoe's or from the way deaf children learn. Koko actually learned two languages at once: sign language, in which she could respond as well as receive messages, and English, in which for a long time she could only receive.

Patterson stayed with Koko in the trailer seven days a week and several nights as well. She spends more hours a day with her gorilla than the field primatologists in Africa spend watching theirs. Koko totally dominates her life. Patterson no longer has free weekends or after-work hours; she spends most of each day either teaching Koko, providing for Koko's material needs, or checking her data on Koko and analyzing the results.

Patterson keeps a daily log or scientific diary, and in it she enters each new sign that either she or another of Koko's tutors teaches her. Koko's progress is also recorded on videotape and film, on which Patterson also records the things that Koko does spontaneously.

By the time Koko was six years old, she weighed 100 pounds. Husky and agile, Koko used her arms as well as her hands to gesture and looked like a small cheerleader as she addressed her tutor. By this time Koko had an Ameslan vocabulary of 300 words.

Meanwhile, Patterson had outfitted the trailer to suit a growing gorilla. Koko's living room is half holding cage. But the rest of the rooms, a kitchen and storeroom, hold normal, though sturdy, appliances and furniture. There used to be an old carpet nailed to the floor, but that has given way to easy-to-clean vinyl.

Gorillas, even baby gorillas, are strong, so chain-link fencing reinforces all the doors. But Koko is free to move about inside as she wishes. The whole trailer is wired with a burglar alarm, which is there to protect Koko from the outside world.

Koko cannot go outside alone, not without permission. The campus is not a zoo, and so her movements are limited. Outdoors

she always wears a chain collar attached to a leash. She occasionally takes walks on the campus. But there Koko always attracts a crowd, so her real outdoor space is limited to a small yard.

She used to have a sandbox in it when she was smaller, and a tricycle. Koko played with children's toys, but like some human children, she also enjoyed teasing the farm animals in the nearby compound. When she lived at the zoo, a stray cat had adopted her, and Koko seemed to enjoy visiting her litter of kittens. Like Congo, she had befriended a house pet. Now, in her own backyard, she likes to chase chickens, rabbits, and goats, and tries to charge a lonely bull. But the farm animals run away, and the bull ignores her. For a long time Koko had to fall back on humans for companionship.

Koko's life at Stanford has been different from that of any other gorilla ever. In some ways she is like a spoiled child, doted on by all who know her, the center of their attention and the focus of their hopes. A typical day in Koko's life is like a human child's day. She eats five regular meals, goes to classes, and has "recesses" when she can play outside. And she takes a lot of tests.

From time to time Patterson gives Koko a standard intelligence test, one that has been especially designed for preschool children who cannot read. But Patterson had to change some of the answers to make it suit a gorilla. Koko was shown five pictures—ice cream, an apple, a block, a shoe, and a flower. Then she was asked to point out which ones are edible. Koko chose the flower and the apple. Patterson considers that the right answer because gorillas do eat flowers.

An IQ score is a general measure of an individual's ability to answer questions in comparison with most people's ability to answer these questions. Children are scored by comparing the number of correct answers they get with the average number of correct answers that children the same age score. If someone is

At six years old, Koko weighed 100 pounds, but she still acted like a baby with her teacher, Penny Patterson. (Stanford University)

five years old and can answer the questions most ten-year-olds can, then that person has a mental age of ten. An IQ is the mental age, divided by the real age, and then multiplied by 100. If a five-year-old can answer all the questions exactly as most five-year-olds can, then that person's IQ is 5, divided by 5, times 100, or 100. 100 is the average IQ.

Koko falls a few months behind the mental age of a human child taking the same tests. Koko's IQ is therefore between 75 and 85. This is below average, but not very far below. Many people who lead normal lives score less than "average" an IQ tests. This

Below: *Koko signs "food," index finger to mouth.* At right: *Koko signs "drink," thumb to mouth.* (Stanford University)

means that if Koko were human, she would be able to get along in the world as well as quite a few of the people in it.

But, Patterson points out, Koko is not human, and she excels in skills that human children cannot do as well. Koko can swing from a bar and climb a tree better than any child her age.

Patterson also tests Koko on her vocabulary. She uses the same system the Gardners used. Koko has to use a sign voluntarily for at least fifteen days in a month for that sign to qualify as learned vocabulary. According to this standard, Koko knew 375 qualified words when she was seven, but she is still learning new signs all the time.

Patterson estimates that Koko knows another 300 words which have not qualified yet, but which are nonetheless part of Koko's working vocabulary.

Koko learned most of these signs through molding. But she has picked up other signs by making them up and by "eavesdropping." She explained to Patterson in February 1978 that she could "sign." Patterson had never taught her the gesture for *sign*. She traced the use of the gesture back to Koko's observing Patterson use it in conversation with one of Koko's deaf tutors. Koko had apparently seen it, understood what it meant, and incorporated it into her own vocabulary.

Koko's signs are not as clear as a human's because her hands are not as flexible as ours. But what she says is indisputable. Koko has confirmed, in Ameslan, what other psychologists have discovered through different kinds of experiments. Koko knows that a

Koko asks for "more" by rubbing her palms together. (Stanford University)

picture of an object is not the same as that object, but is a symbol. She has two words for *flower* in her vocabulary: one for a real flower and one for a picture of a flower. When a visitor arrived wearing a flowered skirt, Koko told her in signs that she eats flowers, but not pictures of flowers.

And when she went to Patterson's off-campus apartment to see herself on television, Koko recognized herself and said so. When she was given a drink from a mug with King Kong's picture on it, she signed that she knew that the picture was a picture of Koko. This is a far cry from Snowflake, who was frightened by his mirror image. But not very different from Muni, who was attracted by his.

Another way to say "more": moving her index finger across her palm (Stanford University)

Koko has already shown that she has a range of ability far beyond what anyone expected. She can start conversations and does not simply wait to be asked questions. In fact, Koko seems to be able to express herself as well as most human children. She can string signs together into sentences when she wants to share experiences, such as "Listen bird." She can demand what she wants, such as refusing a meal of rice bread and pointing, instead, towards the refrigerator and signing "Bottle, there, apple."

She could explain her mood when her tutor finally moved out of the trailer by saying, "Yes, sad cry, morning." But she can also tell her "Me feel fine."

. Koko has shown that she can think abstractly, a skill once thought confined to humans. When she was caught chewing on the sponge with which she had cleaned up a spill—and sponge-chewing is something she is not supposed to do—Patterson confronted her with the remaining sponge and asked Koko what it was. Koko answered "Trouble!" Or when she was caught biting the lead point off her pencil, another forbidden act, Koko pointed to her mouth and signed "teeth," meaning that her teeth were responsible, not Koko.

Koko has also mastered concepts of time, such as "now" and "later." She can express the knowledge that some things are "different" or "same." And she can distinguish colors and is beginning to have a small grasp of numbers.

Following the examples set by Washoe, Koko has also manufactured new words by stringing familiar signs together. She calls a ring a "finger-bracelet," a picture of a zebra a "white tiger," and she signs "eye-hat" to mean mask.

Like Dolly, Koko responds to English. For unlike deaf people who have to rely on Ameslan, Koko can hear, and she is able to understand the spoken words. In June 1977, Patterson developed a device to test Koko's English. She had what looks like a very special typewriter installed in the trailer by Stanford's Institute of Mathematical Studies in the Social Sciences. With forty-six color-coded keys, the "typewriter" is really a computer console. When

Koko presses a button, the computer activates a voice that resounds from a speaker in a monotone.

If Patterson asks Koko what she wants to eat, Koko may sign "catchup" to put on her mashed potatoes. Or she may go to the typewriter and punch the *A* so that the voice says "apple." She may even respond in a phrase, as she did when Patterson offered her a navy bean. Koko rejected it, explaining her action by going to the computer and punching the words "like not."

With two languages, a gesture language and a machine-operated oral language, Koko can express herself well. In the trailer she may prefer the novelty of the computer. Outside she has to depend on her hands. She seems to choose the one she wants to use arbitrarily, but she never mixes them up.

Both of her languages depend on the use of her hands, but she is clever with them. Koko can type with one and sign with the other, for she is ambidextrous as well as bilingual.

Yet even with two languages at her command, Koko is still a gorilla, with gorilla ways. Like Assumbo and Dolly, she hates loud noises and seems impervious to pain. She play-bites as all gorillas do, and when she is very excited, she bites hard. As a small animal she went through a stage of biting the people who came to tutor her. But Patterson stopped that habit before it grew by applying a mild electric shock. Like most wild gorillas, Koko likes to sleep in a nest and makes her own by gathering towels around her on the floor. Like all small gorillas, she loves to play "tickle chase," only Koko *asks* to be tickled.

Another favorite game is her version of blindman's buff. She covers her head with a cloth, then stumbles about the trailer bumping into things. When she can't find a cloth, she just closes her eyes. It seems that this game is universal, not only among human children but among small apes as well.

Like all gorillas, Koko needed a companion of her own species, preferably one of the opposite sex, with whom she could eventually mate. Patterson knew this and started looking for one in 1972. After several false starts, she managed to find a young male gorilla, Michael, who was living in Vienna as a pet. Michael was for sale; his price, $14,000. Penny had to find a way to buy him. Money suddenly loomed as an obstacle to the gorilla project.

The San Francisco Zoo had been generously extending its loan of Koko year after year for five years. But in early 1977, Koko was almost six and would soon enter puberty. Gorillas are rare, expensive, and highly prized zoo animals. In a few years, the zoo hoped Koko would begin having her own babies. And she had to learn to live with her own species if she was to mate. They wanted her back. If not Koko, then, they asked Patterson to find them another female about the same age.

Patterson believes that Koko had gone beyond the point of being able to return to a cage, even the spacious grotto she had left when she was a baby. Patterson also believes that Koko would have died from grief had she been separated from her. Other people have even argued that Koko is no longer an animal now that she has language. They argue that language has turned her into a thinking being who deserves civil rights and protection from arbitrary imprisonment, by which they mean a zoo.

The new zoo director in San Francisco realized that it would be difficult to reintroduce Koko into the grotto after the stimulating life she was used to at Stanford. But he had the zoo's interests to protect. Public money had gone into caring for and breeding Koko's mother, Jackie. They agreed that Patterson could keep Koko if she could pay for her. The price arrived at after some discussion was $12,000.

Patterson, still a graduate student, had no funds of her own to buy Koko and also to pay off the "mortgage" she owed the bank for little Michael. Her scientific research slowed down as she organized a nonprofit foundation, the Gorilla Foundation, dedicated to her gorilla research. By the summer of 1977, the money had been raised and Patterson could return her full attention to the substance of her research.

Michael's arrival changed Koko's life. Two years younger than Koko, he attracted lots of attention, and Koko was certainly jealous. Patterson moved out of the trailer, giving up her room to

Patterson has a snack with Koko and Michael on the Stanford University campus in Palo Alto, California. (Stanford University)

Michael, another blow to Koko. But after a few months, Koko began to protect him and sign for him to accompany her in games and in the play yard. Following Koko's example, Michael was toilet-trained in a month, and he soon learned a dozen signs. He seems as able to learn as Koko, and that is encouraging. Koko's intelligence is proved, but Michael's aptitude, his equal performance on IQ tests, seem to indicate that Koko is no brighter than most other gorillas. She is just the product of a stimulating home. Michael's vocabulary and progress have doubled the scope of the project. Patterson is in a better position now to generalize about gorilla intelligence.

The project has already outgrown Patterson's original plan to see if she could teach a gorilla what the Gardners had taught Washoe. It grew in scope when the computer linkup for the "talking typewriter" was set up. It expanded further with Michael's arrival, and it will expand again when doctors from Stanford's medical school monitor the sleep patterns of both animals. Gorillas have the same REM patterns as humans. There are intervals of Rapid Eye Movement we experience when we are dreaming. Koko has already indicated to Patterson, by waking up crying and screaming in the middle of the night, that she has nightmares. Now Patterson hopes that one day Koko, and Michael too, will be able to tell her about their dreams.

Patterson has already discovered that gorillas learn language very much as humans do. Her evidence, in fact, closely dovetails with what Redshaw revealed through the Piaget tests. Just as gorillas develop cognitive awareness of the outside world as human children do, so Koko and Michael are demonstrating that when these animals are taught a language, they acquire it in the same way: learning the same simple concepts in about the same order.

Patterson believes that the techniques she is developing with Koko and Michael may one day be used in work with young children who are unable to speak and who may be mentally retarded. But whether or not her research is applicable to humans, there is little doubt that she is helping reveal a lot about gorillas.

At seven, Koko's rate of learning seemed to begin to level off. Or it may be, as Patterson believes, that as Koko matures, Patterson may have to find a new measuring technique to keep up with her. Whether or not Koko is still learning as rapidly as before, she has already gone farther than any of the chimpanzees in acquiring language. Patterson hopes to make Koko and Michael a lifelong study. If things work as she plans, and if Koko and Michael produce babies one day, we can look forward to learning even more about gorillas. If Koko retains her vocabulary into maturity, and there is no reason to think she won't, we will learn more about how gorillas feel toward babies, toward each other, and toward *Homo sapiens*.

Patterson's accomplishment with Koko is fascinating. Still unexplained, however, is why such intelligent animals did not develop language on their own. There are people who believe that there cannot be thought without language. This implies that Patterson gave Koko more than words. It would mean that when Patterson gave Koko words, she also gave her the power to think.

Others disagree. They do not link thinking with having a formal language. They argue that the great apes have always been able to communicate with each other through their sounds and gestures. By teaching them our symbols, we have only agreed upon a common vocabulary.

15   The Future

Deep foliage still shelters Papoose on the slope of Mount Visoke, but Uncle Bert is gone, the victim of souvenir hunters who killed him for his head. Papoose may evade the poachers and survive to live out her natural life in the wild. But the fates of succeeding generations of gorillas are less certain. Gorilla populations are dwindling all over Africa, despite some successful efforts of both international conservation groups and individual zealots who are personally fending off poachers and loggers.

The ethologists who are patiently documenting each gorilla's life in the wild refuse to consider any other future. Along with ecologists who are studying the whole biome, they are examining the gorilla as an animal that has evolved special physical attributes as well as a formal pattern of behavior in order to accommodate it-self to these forests. They see the gorillas as an integral part of their habitat.

Other zoologists fear for the future. They are breeding gorillas in captivity to keep the species alive in the event that the forests disappear. They hope that one day, in an enlightened world, humans may be able to reintroduce them into new forest sanctuaries. For the moment, they are anxious to keep gorillas healthy and producing young in Europe, North America, and Japan. And they have already learned a great deal from the data collected by scientists like Fossey, Harcourt, Stewart, and Sabater-Pi.

Half a century ago, captive gorillas seldom survived more than a few months. They usually succumbed to intestinal or lung infections. Many died in the great flu epidemic of 1918, along with thousands of human beings. There are few illnesses, in fact, which humans endure that gorillas do not share. The amino acid molecules in our hemoglobin are almost the same. We have the same blood types. One of the reasons gorillas now survive is that they have benefited from the same medical miracles—antibiotics and vaccines—that are prolonging human lives.

Gorillas resemble humans in more than their chemical and anatomical makeup. That first small captive, Fighting Joe, showed a familiar susceptibility to psychological and emotional stress. Infants like Snowflake, who have passed through the Ikunde Center in Bata, display abnormal behavior soon after they arrive in captivity, vomiting their food and eating it again, along with their own body wastes.

Visitors to zoos all over the world still watch gorillas with these unpleasant habits, unaware that no one has ever seen gorillas behaving that way in the wild. Unhealthy acts, along with what is called *stereotyped behavior,* such as knocking their heads against a wall or scratching a particular patch of fur bare, are familiar in too many bored captive gorillas. Many overeat. Great males in zoos have weighed as much as 200 pounds more than any ever found in the forest.

As psychologists learn more about gorilla intelligence and behavior, they are discovering how to prevent these antisocial actions. The more they understand what is normal in the wild, the more they can help the captives. Certain acts, such as chest beating and nest building, are especially gorilla. Others, such as using tools, are more natural to the other great apes. By studying and comparing the species, scientists are seeking the essence of "gorillaness."

Most of these scientists confess to an emotional bias in favor of gorillas. It was this bias that brought them to their work in the first place. Being aware of it, they feel, ensures it will not interfere with their scientific objectivity and may actually help them in their daily contact with the apes.

Yet all of these projects, even as they aim at exploring the gorilla as a gorilla, lead inexorably to comparing gorillas with other hominoids. It is doubtful that so many scientists would have begun their research had the gorilla been much further removed from humans on the evolutionary scale.

For the gorilla is one of the closest, if not *the* closest, animals to humans. And every single one of these scientists, from du Chaillu through Fossey, Harcourt and Stewart, Sabater-Pi and Riopelle, Yerkes and Redshaw, to Joines, Nadler, and Patterson, is concerned with tracing certain evolutionary characteristics.

Du Chaillu actually sought Joe's "soul," for in every other way he found Joe almost human. Fossey, Harcourt and Stewart have found behavioral patterns in gorilla groups that cannot help but remind us of our own family bonds.

Riopelle's study of Snowflake and Muni reveals a great deal about the nature of leadership and the power of motivation. Yerkes' and later Rumbaugh's tests help us understand the development of intelligence in problem solving. Redshaw's work proves that gorillas and humans develop cognitively in the same way for at least the first eighteen months of life.

Joines and Nadler are just beginning to explore the nature of mothering and nurturing infants: behavior that is still a mystery. They may help us understand those human mothers whom we know, now, abuse their children at least as often as these female gorillas.

And finally, Patterson's work is helping us understand another aspect of thinking—the beginning of language. With Koko's accomplishment, it is hard to deny that gorillas do think.

Evolutionary studies advanced in another area during the 1960s and 1970s. A new field which some call *molecular anthropology* emerged. Unlike fossil hunters who work with objects they can pick up, such as pieces of bone or teeth, in order to draw evolutionary trees, these scientists start with living animals and move backwards. Using chemical analysis, they examine molecules, looking at the sequence of amino acids in protein chains or DNA molecules from two species, and see how they will combine with one another. Or they may see how antibodies in one species react with the proteins in another.

From these comparisons of molecules they often find the same kind of information as the fossil finders. They assume that certain processes, in the past as in the present, take a specific amount of time to occur. From this, then, they believe they can pinpoint when a process occurred and which of the great apes is closest to us.

This approach is new and controversial. The results sometimes disagree with other conclusions, as well as with the speculations of the fossil collectors. But all seem to agree that the modern gorilla is at least as close to us as the chimpanzee, and possibly closer. Studying gorillas is one good way of learning more about human evolution.

Yet neither humans nor gorillas have stopped evolving. One of the questions that disturbs some primatologists is whether the experiments and the breeding programs now under way may be accelerating the rate of change among gorillas. Zoo directors, anxious to increase their stock, are using every possible medical skill to save animals that would probably die in the wild. And despite the growing number of gorilla births, the gene pool is small. A few male animals, such as Jambo, who is now at Jersey, and Trib in San Diego, are the fathers of many of the new generation.

They wonder if this concentration of genetic material in a small number of not-always-healthy animals is producing a new gorilla. They wonder if the games and television that entertain Assumbo, or Koko's languages, are replacing the gorilla's behavioral inheritance with a new kind of behavior better suited to captivity.

If this is happening, are we losing touch with the real gorilla and helping produce a new animal? Will this new creature be lost in that hoped-for future, when new forest enclaves are ready to welcome him back? Would the reintroduced gorilla look around and take the next plane back to San Diego?

All this is speculation. But it is hard to avoid fantasizing about the future. We already know that gorillas can think and do indeed think, whether or not they tell us their thoughts. Yerkes suspected that Miss Congo knew something she was not revealing, that she had a special cunning. He would probably have agreed that although gorillas clearly are not people, they are not actually animals either.

BIBLIOGRAPHY

All the works listed below contributed to this book. Most of them may not be readily available to the general reader. Of those works that are available, the ones preceded by an asterisk (*) are especially recommended.

ARTICLES

Burbridge, Juanita Case. "Miss Congo." *Nature Magazine* (August 1926).

Carter, Stephen F. "Comparison of Baby Gorillas with Human Infants." *Jersey Wildlife Preservation Trust Annual Report*. Jersey, Channel Islands (1973).

Cousins, Don. "The Breeding of Gorillas, *Gorilla gorilla,* in Zoological Collections." *Zoological Garten N. F.,* vol. 46. Leipzig (1976).

————. "Censuses of Gorillas in Zoological Collections with Notes on Numerical Status and Conservation." *International Zoo News,* no. 137 (1976).

————. "Gorillas in Captivity Past and Present." *Zoological Garten N. F.,* vol. 42. Leipzig (1972).

Fossey, Dian. "Observations on the Home Range of One Group of Mountain Gorillas (*Gorilla gorilla beringei*)." *Animal Behavior,* vol. 22 (1974).

————. "Vocalizations of the Mountain Gorilla." *Animal Behavior,* vol. 20 (1972).

————, A. H. Harcourt and K. S. Stewart. "Male Emigration and Female Transfer in Wild Mountain Gorilla." *Nature,* vol. 263 (1976).

Groves, Colin P. "Asymmetry in Gorilla Skulls: Evidence of Lateralized Brain Function?" *Nature,* vol. 244 (1973).

————. "Distribution and Place of Origin of the Gorilla." *Man,* vol. 6, no. 1 (1971).

————. "Population Systematics of the Gorilla." *Journal of the Zoological Society of London,* vol. 161 (1970).

Gwynne, Peter, Steven Michaud, James Pringle and Peter Greenberg. "Almost Human." *Newsweek* (March 7, 1977).

Harcourt, A. H. "Virunga Gorillas—The Case Against Translocations." *Oryx* (1976).

Hayes, Harold T. P. "The Pursuit of Reason." *The New York Times Magazine* (June 12, 1977).

Joines, Steven. "The Gorilla Conservation Program at the San Diego Wild Animal Park." *Zoonooz* (October 1976).

————, Patricia Schollay, Catherine Baldridge and Americo Cuzzone. "Learning to Be a Mother." *Zoonooz* (April 1975).

Jonch, Antonio. "The White Lowland Gorilla." *International Zoo Yearbook,* vol. 8 (1968).

Mallinson, Jeremy J. C., Phillip Coffey and Jeremy Usher-Smith. "Maintenance, Breeding and Hand-rearing of Lowland Gorilla." *Jersey Wildlife Preservation Trust Annual Report.* Jersey, Channel Islands (1973).

Nadler, Ronald D. "Determinants of Variability in Maternal Behavior of Captive Female Gorillas." *Symposium of the 5th Congress of the International Primate Society* (1974).

————. "Periparturitional Behavior of a Primparous Lowland Gorilla." *Primates* (March 1974).

————. "Second Gorilla Birth at the Yerkes Regional Primate Center." *International Zoo Yearbook,* vol. 15 (1975).

————. "Three Gorillas Born at Yerkes in One Month." *Yerkes Newsletter,* vol. 13 (1976).

———— and Susan Green. "Separation and Reunion of a Gorilla Infant and Mother." *International Zoo Yearbook,* vol. 15 (1975).

Ravenstern, E. G. "Obituary—Paul Belloni du Chaillu." London: *Geographic Journal* (1903).

Redshaw, Margaret. "Breeding, Hand-rearing and Development of the Third Lowland Gorilla." *Jersey Wildlife Preservation Trust Annual Report.* Jersey, Channel Islands (1974).

————. "Cognitive, Manipulative and Social Skills in Gorillas: Part II, The Second Year." *Jersey Wildlife Preservation Trust Annual Report*. Jersey, Channel Islands (1975).

———— and Jennifer Hughes. "The Psychological Development of Two Infant Gorillas: A Preliminary Report." *Jersey Wildlife Preservation Trust Annual Report*. Jersey, Channel Islands (1973).

———— and Karen Locke. "The Development of Play and Social Behavior in Two Lowland Gorilla Infants." *Jersey Wildlife Preservation Trust Annual Report*. Jersey, Channel Islands (1976).

Riopelle, Arthur J. "Development and Behavior of the White Gorilla." *National Geographic Society Research Reports* (1968).

———— and Clyde Jones. "Field Studies of Primates in Río Muni, West Africa, 1967–1968." *National Geographic Society Research Report* (1968).

———— and K. Kuk. "Growing Up with Snowflake." *National Geographic*, vol. 138 (1970).

————, R. Nos and A. Jonch. "Situational Determinants of Dominance in Captive Young Gorillas." *Proceedings Third International Congress Primatology*, vol. 3 (1970).

———— and Paul A. Zahl. "Snowflake: The World's First White Gorilla." *National Geographic*, vol. 131 (1967).

Rumbaugh, Duane M. "The Birth of a Lowland Gorilla at the San Diego Zoo." *Zoonooz* (September 1965).

———— and Timothy Gill. "The Learning Skills of Great Apes." *Journal of Human Evolution* (1972).

———— and Carol McCormack. "Great Ape Intelligence." *Zoonooz* (July 1967).

———— and Carol McCormack. "Learning Skills of Anthropoids." *Primate Behavior Developments in Field and Laboratory Research*, edited by Leonard A. Rosenblum, vol. 1. New York: Academic Press (1970).

Sabater-Pi, Jorge. "An Albino Gorilla from Río Muni, West Africa." *Folia Primatologia*, vol. 7 (1967).

————. "Aportacio a una Ecologia de la Alimentación en Estado Natural de Los Gorillas de Costa." *Ethnica, Revista de Antropologia Barcelona*, no. 10 (1975).

————. "Las Camas de Los Gorillas Apuntes a su Estudio." *Revista Zoo*, no. 26 (July 1976).

Sacher, W., A. S. Weiner, A. S. Moon-Jankowski and J. Mortelmans. "Blood Groups of Mountain Gorillas." *Journal of Medical Primatology* (1973).

Sarich, Vincent. "A Molecular Approach to the Question of Human Origins." *Annals*. New York Academy of Sciences (1962).

Thomas, Warren D. "Hail Caesar!!" *Zoo View* (1977).

BOOKS

*Amon, Aline. *Reading, Writing, Chattering Chimps*. New York: Atheneum, 1975.

*Bourne, Geoffrey. *Primate Odyssey*. New York: G. P. Putnam's Sons, 1974.

*———— and Maury Cohen. *The Gentle Giants: The Gorilla Story*. New York: G. P. Putnam's Sons, 1975.

Browne, Alexander Montagu. *Artistic and Scientific Taxidermy and Modelling*. London: A. & C. Black, 1896.

Burbridge, Ben. *Gorilla*. London: George G. Harrap & Co., Ltd., 1928.

Chance, M., and C. Jolly. *Social Groups and Monkeys, Apes and Man*. New York: E. P. Dutton, 1970.

Dolhinow, Phyllis, ed. *Primate Patterns*. New York: Holt, Rinehart and Winston, 1972.

du Chaillu, Paul B. *Exploration & Adventures in Equatorial Africa*. London: John Murray, 1861.

————. *A Journey to Shangoland*. New York: Appleton and Co., 1867.

————. *Stories of the Gorilla Country*. London: William Clowes and Sons, 1868.

Garner, Richard Lynche. *Gorillas and Chimpanzees*. London: Osgood and McIlvaine, 1896.

Goodman, Morris, and Richard E. Tashian, eds. *Molecular Anthropology*. New York: Plenum Press, 1976.

Griffin, Donald R. *The Question of Animal Awareness: Evolutionary Awareness of Mental Experience*. New York: Rockefeller University Press, 1956.

Gunther, Albert E. *A Century of Zoology*. London: Dawsons of Pall Mall, 1975.

*Hahn, Emily. *On the Side of the Apes*. New York: Crowell, 1971.

*Jolly, Alison. *The Evolution of Primate Behavior*. New York: Macmillan, 1972.

*Kevles, Bettyann. *Watching the Wild Apes: The Primate Studies of Goodall, Fossey, and Galdikas*. New York: E. P. Dutton, 1976.

*Linden, Eugene. *Apes, Men and Language*. New York: Saturday Review Press, E. P. Dutton, 1974.

*Reynolds, Vernon. *The Apes*. New York: E. P. Dutton, 1967.

*Rosen, S. I. *Introduction to the Primates: Living and Fossil*. Englewood Cliffs, N.J.: Prentice-Hall, Inc., 1974.

Royal Geographic Society. *Proceedings*. 1873, 1874.

*Schaller, George B. *The Year of the Gorilla*. Chicago: University of Chicago Press, 1964.

*Simonds, Paul E. *The Social Primates*. New York: Harper & Row, 1974.

*Simons, Elwyn. *Primate Evolution*. New York: Macmillan, 1972.

Wendt, Herbert. *From Ape to Adam: The Search for the Ancestry of Man*. New York: Bobbs, Merrill Company, Inc., 1972.

Yerkes, Robert M. *The Mind of a Gorilla*. Worcester, Massachusetts: Clark University, 1927.

———— and Ada W. *The Great Apes: A Study of Anthropoid Life*. New Haven: Yale University Press, 1929.

MAGAZINES

The Atheneum. London, 1861, 1862.

Journal. Royal Geographic Society. 1861.

Zoonooz. San Diego, 1973.

NEWSLETTER

"The Great Apes: A Dialogue with Louis Leakey Protégées Goodall, Fossey, Galdikas-Brindamour." *L. S. B. Leakey Foundation News, Great Apes Supplement* (1976).

INDEX

Italic page numbers refer to captions.

abstract thinking ability, 144
Afenengui, 63–64
aframomun shrub, 52–53
Africa
  central, map of, 5
  gorilla habitats in, 2–4, 11–12
age, learning ability and, 82
Akeley, Carl and Mary, 28
Albert National Park, 28, 38
American Museum of Natural History, 28
Assumbo, 85–107, *89, 99, 103,* 134
Augustus, 34, 36, 39, 112

Bamenda, *91*
Barcelona Zoo, 49, 56, *59*
Belgian Congo, 28, 66
Bible, 8
Binet, Alfred, 70
Binti, 115–116, *116, 125,* 126
biome, 3, 52, 150

body language, 131
brain:
  gorilla vs. human, 20–21, 74–75, 84, 90
  laterality of, 75
British Geographical Society, 18, 22
Brutus, 118
Burbridge, Ben, 67–70, 71, 72, 73
Burbridge, Juanita, 68–69, 71

Caesar, 118–119, *120, 121*
Cameroon, 4, 11
Cameroons, 3, 87
cause and effect, understanding of, 96–97
Central Park Zoo (New York City), 68, 124, 128
chimpanzees, 2, 7, 29, 48, 52, 58, 69, 71, 74, 75, 81, 82, 84, 131

chimpanzees (*continued*)
    human communication with, 131,
        132–133
computers
    in ethological research, 39
    in language learning, 133, 144–
        145, 148
concentration, as mental ability, 81
Congo, 3, 4, 128
Congo (gorilla), 66–84, *77, 78, 79,*
    133, 138, 154
    Yerkes' study of intelligence of,
        71–72, 73–82
Congo River, 2, 4, 10, 14
curiosity, as mental ability, 71, 80
Cuzzone, Ricky, 113

Darwin, Charles, 8
Delta Regional Primate Facility
    (Louisiana), 49
Descent of Man, The (Darwin), 8
developmental stages, Piaget's
    theory of, 92–93, 94, 148
Dolly, 108–116, *108, 114, 116,*
    125–126, *125,* 144
Dryopithecus, 2
du Chaillu, Paul Belloni, 14–25, *23,*
    152
    as taxidermist, 19–21
    travel books by, 23–24, *24*
Durrell, Gerald, 85

East Midland Zoological Society,
    Twycross (England), 104, 106
ecology, 3, 11–12, 52, 150
Ellie, 117–120, *119*
Emory University, 83, 120–121
Equatorial Guinea, Republic of, 4,
    48
ethology, 29, 39, 150
evolution
    of abilities, 83, 93, 102, 148, 152

evolution (*continued*)
    dominance and, 59
    gorilla's place in, 8, 12, 152, 153
    molecular studies in, 153
experiments, measurements, and
    tests
    on dominance roles, 60–64
    of gorilla vs. human brain-skull
        development, 90
    in language learning, 131, 132–
        149
    in pre- and post-natal behavior,
        120–122
    by Redshaw of development,
        90–107
    by Yerkes, of gorilla intelligence,
        72, 73–84
    by Yerkes, of primate intelli-
        gence, 70–72
explorers, nineteenth-century, 17–
    18

Fanya, 123
Fighting Joe, *see* Joe
Fort Gorilla (Congo), 128, *129*
Fossey, Dian, 29–31, 35, 38, 39,
    41, 75, 151, 152

Gabon, 4, 7, 14, 17
Gardner, Allen and Beatrice, 132–
    133, 136, 137
Garner, Richard L., 128–130, *129*
gestures as communication, 131–
    132
Gombe Stream (Tanzania), 29
Goodall, Jane, 29
Gorilla Foundation, 146
Gorilla gorilla beringei, 4, 28, 46
Gorilla gorilla gorilla, 4, 28, 87
Gorilla gorilla graueri, 4

gorillas
  abnormal behavior of, 118–120, 134, 151
  adaptations of, 3, 11, 52, 150, 153–154
  aggression of, 34–35
  albino, 48, 56, 65
  anatomy of vs. human anatomy, 19, 20–21, *22,* 74–75, 89–90, 131–132, 151
  behavior of vs. human behavior, 70, 80–82, 83–84, 90, 91–93, 94–107, *103,* 131–132, 139–141, 145, 148–149, 151–152
  births in captivity, 86–87, 107, 111, 117–120, 122–124, 126, 127
  bonding between, 45, 123
  captivity and, 7, 14–17, 28, 53–55, 68–70, 87, 124, 151, 153–154
  chest beating by, 34, 53, 104, 111, 151
  conservation of, 11–12, 28, 46, 49, 50, 87, 112, 126, 134, 150–151
  daily life of, in wild, 31–33, 52
  developmental stages of, 94–97, 100, 102, *103,* 148
  diet of, 3, 21, 26, 27, 33, 40, 50, 52
  ecology of, 11–12, 150
  emotional responses of, 17, 32, 72, 81, 144, 146, 151
  as endangered species, 11–12, 27–28, 46, 50, 87, 134, 150–151
  Europeans' early attitudes toward, 6–10, *10,* 25
  facial expressions of, 45, 104
  family patterns of, 35–36, 45–46, 124–125, 152

gorillas (*continued*)
  feeding by, 27, 32–33
  feet of, 21, *22*
  females, behavior of, 20, 33–34, 35–36, 39, 45
  as firstborn infants, special risks of, 123
  friendships of, 33, 39
  genetic pool of, 153
  grooming among, 43–44
  group life of, 11, 26–27, 33–36, 38, 39–46, 52
  habitats of, 2–4, 11–12
  as habituated to humans, 27, 29, 31, 38
  hair (pelage; fur) of, 4, 15, 19, 31
  hands of, 21, *22*
  health of, 31, 40, 54, 124, 127, 151
  hierarchy of, 41, 65
  hunting of, 9–11, 13–14, 50, 66–67, 150
  identification (nose-prints) of, 30–31, 46
  infant deaths of, in wild, 35, 40
  insight demonstrated by, 76–79, 81–82, 83
  knuckle pads of, 21
  "language" of, 128–130
  language taught to, 134–135, 136–149, *140, 142*
  leader's role among, 32, 33, 38, 45, 58–65, 152
  legends and superstitions about, 1, 6, 7, 11, 17, 25, 38, 48
  lowland, 3, 4, 5, 11, 15, 28, 49–65, 87, *125*
  males, behavior of, 20, 34–35, 39, 45
  mating patterns of, 35, 40–41, 45
  mental ability of, 70–72, 73–84, *77, 79,* 92–93, 94–102, 133, 139–141, 144, 147, 151, 152

gorillas (*continued*)
  migration of females among, 34–35, 45
  mother-infant relationships among, in captivity, 84, 85–86, 111–116, 117–120, 122–126, 152
  mountain, 3, 4, *4*, 11, 26–46
  mountain vs. lowland, 50, 52, 53
  nests of, 17, 27, 33, 40, 50, 52, 53, 57, 145, 151
  nostril shapes of, 4, *6*, 21, 31
  nuchal ridges of, 20
  origin of, 2–3
  other apes compared with, 71, 74, 75, 80, 81, 82–84, 151–152
  personality differences among, 57–58, 72, 81, 88–89
  physical characteristics of, 4, *4*, 15, 19–21, 30–31, 90, 98, 107, 130, 131, 133
  physical differences among, 3, 4, 20, 26, 31, 75
  physical skills of, 71–72, 73–74, 80, 92–93, 94–102
  play of, 32, 54, 58, 97, 104–106, 108, 145
  range of, 31, 38, 52
  sagittal crests of, 20, 90
  sexuality studies of, 121
  as silverbacks (mature leaders), 15, 26, 32, 45, 58
  sleep patterns of, 148
  social relationships of, 33, 39, 41, 43–45, 58–65, 88–90, 97, 104–106, 110–116, 123–126, 145–147
  sounds (communication and social) of, 13, 27, 29, 31, 34, 52, 53, 57, 104, 122, 128–129
  species classification of, 3, 4–5, 7
  stereotyped behavior of, 151

gorillas (*continued*)
  television watching by, 106, 143
  thinking ability ascribed to, 82, 144, 149, 152, 154
  vision of, 20
gravity, understanding of, 96
great apes, *see* chimpanzees; gorillas; orangutans
Groves, Colin, 2–3

handedness, 74–75
hand-eye coordination, 96
Hanno, 7
Harcourt, Alexander H. (Sandy), 30–31, *30*, 37–46, 123, 151, 152
  check sheets of, research, 41–42, *42–43*, 44
  maps of, circle, 44–45, *44*
Harlow, Harry and Margaret, 83
Hominoidea, 7
Howletts Zoo (England), 100
Hunt, J. M., 95

Ikunde Animal Acclimatization Center (Equatorial Africa), 49, 53–54
imitation, as mental ability, 81
insight, meaning of, 76, 83
International Trade in Endangered Species Convention (1973), 11
IQ tests, 70, 139–141

Jackie, 127, 146
Jambo, 87, 100, 153
Jersey Wildlife Preservation Trust (Channel Islands), 85–87, *91*, 94, 104
Jim, 111, 112, 113, 125–126, *125*
Joe (Fighting Joe), 13–25, 151, 152
Johnson, Osa and Martin, 82

Joines, Steven, 113–115, 152
Jones, Clyde, 49, 50–52

Kahuzi-Biega National Park
(Zaire), 31
Karisoke Research Center, (Rwanda), 29–31, 38, 130
research procedure at, 39–40,
41–45, *42–43, 44,* 46
Kaye-Sonogram technique, 130
Kigoma (Belgian Congo), 28
Kishina, 122
Kivu, Lake (Rwanda), 3, 29, 37
Köhler, Wolfgang, 71, 76
Koko (Hanabi-Ko), 127–128, 134–
135, 136–149, *140, 142, 143,
147,* 152
Ameslan and English learned by,
134–135, 136–149
Kongo, 124–125

Lana, 133
language
computers used in teaching of,
133, 144–145, 148
gestures as, 131–132
learning of, by apes, 130–149
new form of (Yerkish), 133
speech vs., 130
studies of, in wild, 128–130
thinking ability and, 149, 152
learning sets, 83
licking, as bonding mechanism, 123
Livingstone, David, 17
Los Angeles Zoo, 117, *119, 120,
121*
Lulu, 124–125

Mamfe, 88–107, *89, 103, 106,* 134
Mané, Benito, 47, 48
Marzo, 67, 68
memory, as mental ability, 81

Michael, 146–148, *147*
Mikeno, Mount, *4*
Mind of a Gorilla, The (Yerkes), 72
molding, in sign language, 136–
137, 142
molecular anthropology, 153
Moro reflex, 90
motivation, dominance and, 63–65,
152
Muni, 57–65, *59, 61,* 143, 152
mutualism, 52–53

Nadler, Ronald D., 122–124, 125,
152
Nandi, 85–86, 87, 100
Ndengue, 65
Nevada, University of, 132
Nigeria, 4
Nko rain forest, 47
N'Pongo, 87, 88, 100
Nunki, 34–35

object permanence, 95–96, 103
(chart)
observations, scientific
of ape "language" in wild,
128–130, 131
as field primatology (or ethology), 29
of mother-newborn relationship,
88–89, 117–118, 121–123
in wild, 27, 28, 29, 38–46, 150
see also experiments, measurements, and tests
Oliver, 95–97, 100, *100, 103,* 107
operant conditioning, maternal care
and, 113–116
Orange Park, Florida, primate laboratory, 82
orangutans, 7, 70–71, 74, 75, 81,
82, 84, 108, *110*
Origin of Species (Darwin), 8

Othello, 130
Owen, Richard, 7

Paki, 120–124
Papoose, 26–36, 39, 112, 150
Parc des Volcans (Rwanda), 26
Patterson, Francine (Penny), 128,
    134–135, 136–149, *147*, 152
Patty Cake, 124–125
Petula, 33, 34, 35, 39, 112
Piaget, Jean, 92, 94
Pongidae, 7
Pribram, Karl H., 135
primatology, 2–3, 18, 29, 153
psychobiology, 70
psychology, 11, 70–71, 83
Punch, 9, *10*

Redshaw, Margaret, 90–107, *91*,
    134, 148
reflections, concept of, 60–61, *61*,
    106, 112, 143
Reuther, Ronald, 134–135
Ringling, John, circus of, 72
Río Muni, 47, 48, *50*
Riopelle, Arthur, 49, 56–57, 60,
    152
Roberta, 110, *110*
Ruhengeri (Rwanda), 29, 37
Rumbaugh, Duane, 83–84, 133,
    152
Rwanda, 4, 11, 26, 29, 37

Sabater-Pi, Jorge, 49, 50–53, *50*,
    151
Sam, 95–97, 100, *100, 103*, 107
Samson, 35
San Diego Zoo, 83, 108, 110, *110*,
    112
San Francisco Zoo, 127, 134–135,
    146
Savage, Thomas, 7

Schaller, George B., 28–29, 39, 41
sexual dimorphism, 20
Sign Language, American (Ames-
    lan), 132–133, 134, 136–149,
    140, 142, 143
Snowflake, 47–65, *48, 55, 59, 62,
    64*, 143, 151, 152
speech
    anatomy and, 131–132
    of animals, in folklore, 128
    language vs., 130
Stanford University, 128, 135, 145,
    147
Stewart, Kelly, 30–31, *30*, 39, 46,
    123, 151, 152

"talking typewriter," 144–145, 148
Tanganyika, Lake, 29, 66
Tanzania, 29
Tatu, *102, 103, 105*
taxidermy, 19–21
Tenerife (Canary Islands), 71
Trib, 108, *110*, 112, *125*, 153

Uganda, 4, 11
Uncle Bert, 33–36, 39, 43–44, 150
Usher-Smith, Jeremy, 86, 98, 105
Uzgiris, I. C., 95

Vila, 111, *125*, 126
Virunga Mountains, 3, 4, 28, 29,
    31, 37, 50
Visoke, Mount (Rwanda), 29, 39,
    49
visual perception, 83
visual pursuit, 95, 103 (chart)
von Beringe, Oscar, 28

Washoe, 132–133, 136, 137, 144
Whinney, 26, 27, 30, 33

Wild Animal Park (San Diego Zoo), 110, 125, *125*
Wyman, Jeffries, 7

Yale University, 82
Year of the Gorilla, The (Schaller), 29
Yerkes, Ada, 80
Yerkes, Robert Mearns, 70–83, 133, 152, 154

Yerkes Regional Primate Center, 83, 120, 123, 133
Yerkish language, 133

Zaire, 4, 11, 31, 39, 108
Zaire (gorilla), *102, 103*
zoology, 17–18, 25, 150–151
zoos, 9–10, 12, 28, 46, 49, 56, *59,* 67, 68, 83, 85, 87, 104, 110, 112, 117, 126, 127, 151
primate centers vs., 120